Surrey
Teashop Walks

Jean Patefield

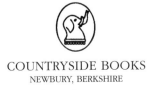

COUNTRYSIDE BOOKS
NEWBURY, BERKSHIRE

COUNTRYSIDE BOOKS
3 Catherine Road
Newbury, Berkshire

To view our complete range of books,
please visit us at
www.countrysidebooks.co.uk

ISBN 1 85306 773 3

Designed by Graham Whiteman
Cover illustration by Colin Doggett
Photographs and maps by the author

Typeset by Textype, Cambridge
Produced through MRM Associates Ltd., Reading
Printed by Woolnough Bookbinding Ltd., Irthlingborough

Contents

Walk

Walk

KEY TO SKETCH MAPS

Path on route	– – →	Teashop	☕
Path not on route	• • •	Pub referred to in text	PH
Road	═══	Point in text	⑤
River, Stream or canal	∿∿∿	Car park	▢
Sea, lake or pond	〜〜	Building or feature referred to in text	■
Summit	▲	Railway	++++++
Church	†		

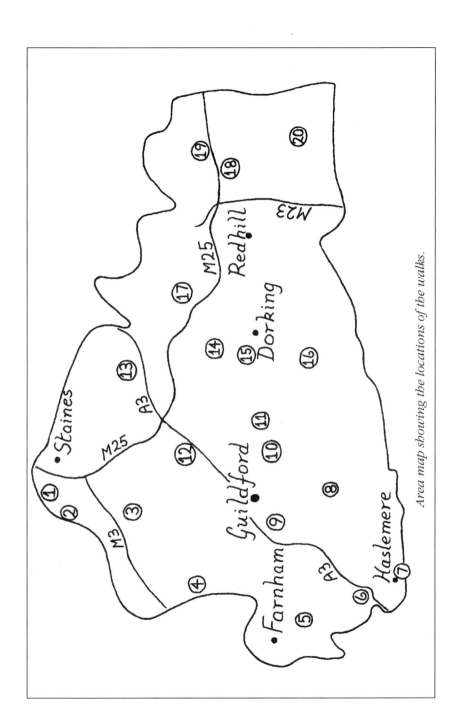

Area map showing the locations of the walks.

Introduction

Surrey has some of the best walking country in Southern England. Thousands of miles of footpaths lead through woods and across heaths and fields to breathtaking viewpoints. Almost every walk in this book has good views but Leith Hill (Walk 16), Newlands Corner (Walk 10) and Cooper's Hill (Walk 1) are outstanding. Black Down (Walk 7) is in Sussex, but most of the route is in Surrey and so it is included in this volume.

The view of Surrey as a commuter dormitory criss-crossed by motorways could not be further from the truth. In fact, Surrey is the most heavily wooded county in England with some 20% of its area covered with trees, often carefully protected (Walk 19). If you enjoy walking in the woods, this is the book for you.

Two ranges of hills cross Surrey roughly west to east. To the north are the North Downs. These are made of chalk and support downland vegetation, a mixture of grasses and low plants, which is maintained by grazing. It is a delight to walk across, especially in summer when the flowers are out (Walk 11).

Further south is the higher Greensand Ridge, including Leith Hill (Walk 16), the highest point in south-east England. This falls short of the 1,000 feet needed to make it a mountain, but the tower built on its summit takes it to over that height and includes a teashop! The greensand is less fertile and traditional agriculture led to the development of heath, dominated by ferns, gorse and heather. In recent years the decline in grazing has allowed trees to invade, notably Scots pine, which was also deliberately planted in some cases. The scent of the pines on a warm summer's day is a heady experience. Lowland heath supports many rare species and is a much-threatened habitat. The National Trust and others are making strenuous efforts to conserve what is left (Walk 3 and Walk 7).

In earlier times, much of Surrey was a poor backwater, and its cathedral at Guildford was only completed in the 20th century. The hills, heaths and forest made travel difficult and dangerous (Walk 3 and Walk 12) and the farming by and large is not rich. Unlike neighbouring Kent and Sussex, it is not on the frontier and no significant battles were fought over its acres. There are no castles and no forts but there are beautiful gardens (Walk 2 and Walk 13). There was an important iron industry until the lack of coal and patriotism (Walk 20) took it away to more northern reaches of the kingdom. To think that nothing much happened, however, would be wrong. People lived their lives and left a legacy of attractive villages (Walk 11 and Walk 5) and events in Surrey shaped our modern democracy (Walk 1).

Tea is often said to be the best meal to eat out in England and I believe that it is something to be enjoyed on all possible occasions. The custom of afternoon tea is said to have been invented by Anna, Duchess of Bedford, in about 1840. She often became peckish in the late afternoon – don't we all? – and invited her friends to join her in a snack of sandwiches and cake. Scones with clotted cream and strawberry jam, delicious home-made cakes, toasted teacakes dripping with butter in winter, delicate cucumber sandwiches in summer, all washed down with the cup that cheers, are some of the best, typically English food available and often excellent value. Bad for the figure maybe, but the walking will see to that.

The best teashops serve a range of cakes, all home-made and including fruit cake, as well as scones and other temptations. Also, teapots should be capacious and pour properly. Most of the teashops visited on these walks fulfil all these criteria admirably and they all offer a good cup of tea. They always have at least light lunches available as well so there is no need to think of these walks as just something for the afternoons.

There is an abundance of excellent establishments in Surrey but, even so, teashops are not scattered evenly throughout the county. In some places popular with tourists, the visitor is spoilt for choice. In such cases the most convenient teashop that, in the author's opinion, most closely fulfils the criteria set out above is recommended but should that not appeal, there are others from which to choose. In other places where there is a delightful walk to be enjoyed, the choice for tea is more limited. However, I have always been able to offer you a good tea partway round an attractive walk. The opening times and telephone number of each teashop are given. Some are rather vague about when they open out of season: it seems to depend on weather and mood. If you are planning a walk on a wet November Tuesday, for example, a call to check that tea will actually be available that day is a wise precaution. A few are definitely closed in the depths of winter and for these walks, where possible, an alternative source of refreshment is given. In most cases, these are pubs serving food, which in some cases includes tea.

The pleasures of summer walking are obvious. Many of the teashops featured in this book have an attractive garden where tea can be taken outside when the weather is suitable. However, let me urge you not to overlook the pleasures of a good walk in winter. The roads and paths are quieter and what could be better than sitting by an open fire in a cosy teashop scoffing crumpets that you can enjoy with a clear conscience due to the brisk walk to get them!

The 20 walks in this book explore the varied landscapes of Surrey. They are all between 3 and 7½ miles long and should be well within the capacity of the average person, including those of mature years and families with children. They are intended to take the walker through this attractive corner of England at a gentle pace with plenty of time to stop and stare, to savour the beauty and interest all around. A dedicated yomper and stomper could probably knock off the whole book in a single weekend but in doing so they would have missed the point and seen nothing. To fully appreciate the countryside it is necessary to go slowly with your eyes and ears open.

Some of the walks are short and level, ideal for a pipe opener on a winter's day, or giving plenty of time to dawdle away a summer's afternoon. Others are longer or more strenuous, some making an excellent all-day expedition. Certain of the walks involve some climbing. This is inevitable as hills add enormous interest to the countryside and with no hills there are no views. However, this presents no problem to the sensible walker who has three uphill gears – slowly, very slowly and admiring the view.

All the routes are on public rights of way or permissive paths and have been carefully checked but, of course, in the countryside things do change; a stile replaces a gate or a wood is extended. A sketch map illustrates each walk and they are all circular. An Ordnance Survey map is useful as well, especially for identifying the main features of views. The Explorer 1:25,000 (2½ inches to 1 mile) series provides by far the best maps to use for walking. Sheets 133, 145, 146, 160 and 161 cover the walks in this book. The grid reference of the starting point and the appropriate maps are given for each walk.

Of course, it behoves us all to remember that the place where we take our recreation is other people's workplace and act with consideration to those who depend on the countryside for their livelihood and make their homes there.

The walks are designed so that, starting where suggested, the teashop is reached in the second half so a really good appetite for tea can be worked up and then its effects walked off. Some walks start at a car park, which is ideal. Where this is not possible, the suggested starting place will always have somewhere where a few cars can be left without endangering other traffic or causing inconvenience. However, it sometimes fits in better with the plans for the day to start and finish at the teashop and for each walk there are details of how to do this.

So put on your walking shoes and prepare to be delighted by the charms of Surrey and refreshed by a traditional English tea!

Jean Patefield

Walk 1
COOPER'S HILL AND RUNNYMEDE

This is a walk to reflect on the impact of past events on our lives today as it passes memorials to three significant events. It also has extensive views, much wildlife interest and the chance to literally visit the United States of America! From the top of Cooper's Hill you can see seven counties. This panorama is not gained without some effort but the modest expenditure of energy needed is amply rewarded and justifies a good tea at an excellent teashop. The return leg after tea is a gentle and interesting stroll by the river Thames.

Magna Carta Tea Rooms is housed in one of a pair of lodges designed by Sir Edwin Lutyens and built in memory of Lord Fairhaven whose wife and sons gave the Meads to the National Trust in 1931. They serve a delicious selection of cakes and other teatime goodies. For a light lunch, sandwiches are always available and daily specials, which change with the seasons. The hours vary a bit depending on the time of year but they are open between 9.30 am and 4 pm all year, later in the summer. Telephone: 01784 477110.

DISTANCE: 3 miles.

MAP: OS Explorer 160 Windsor, Weybridge and Bracknell.

STARTING POINT: The car park at Runnymede Pleasure Grounds (charge) (GR 008723). There is also a free car park on Cooper's Hill near the Air Forces Memorial.

HOW TO GET THERE: The starting point is on the A308 Windsor to Staines road, about ½ mile west of the M25 (junction 13).

ALTERNATIVE STARTING POINT: If you wish to visit the teashop at the beginning or end of your walk, start at the National Trust car park (charge) about ½ mile west of the Pleasure Grounds car park. The teashop is across the road. You will then start the walk at point 7.

THE WALK

1. Leave the rear of the car park and walk to the bank of the river Thames. Turn right.

2. Turn right on a track at the end of a large, dark green building. This shortly leads to the main road. Cross the road to a stile and then take a path straight ahead across a meadow then continue with a hedge on the right. Bear left at a fork and make for a footbridge seen ahead, turn right across it, and continue to a gate and second footbridge on the left.

These are water meadows, as you will find out if you do this walk during or after a wet winter. The soil is rich, fertilised by material carried downstream by the river and deposited in the flood plain. It is grazed and mown for hay and supports a diverse and colourful community of wild flowers. These in turn are the food of many insects and birds, including skylarks whose song can be heard above the drone of the M25.

3. Go through the gate and head up the slope to a second gate onto a track.

4. Turn right along the track until it bends sharply left.

This is Cooper's Hill. The best views are from the Air Forces Memorial.

To visit this reminder of the sacrifice made by 20,000 aircrew, continue along the track as it becomes a road. Follow it round to the right to the entrance on the right. There are some steps to the top of the tower. When you are ready, retrace your steps and continue from point 5.

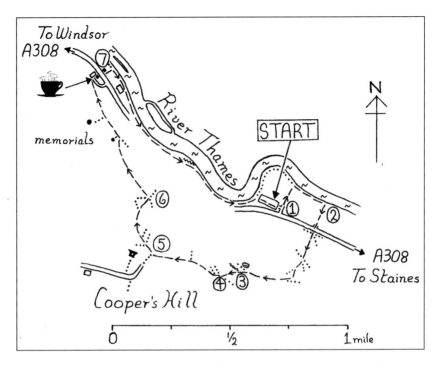

To Windsor
A308

memorials

River Thames

START

N

memorials

⑦

⑥

⑤

④③

①②

A308
To Staines

Cooper's Hill

0   ½   1 mile

This powerful memorial was opened by Queen Elizabeth II in 1953 and is dedicated to the aircrew of the Commonwealth nations who have no known grave. It is a sobering experience to read the lists of names on the walls, some of whom died in a conflict half a world away from their homeland. When she opened the memorial, the Queen quoted the words of the poet Pope, which proved particularly apt:

*'On Cooper's Hill eternal wreaths shall grow
While lasts the mountain or while the Thames shall flow.'*

5. Take a path on the bend through a gate and follow the stepped path down through woodland, ignoring all paths to left and right, to the bottom of the hill and the edge of the woodland.

The name Cooper's Hill comes from the Cowper family. After the Conquest they were well known for defying the oppressive forest law brought in by the conquering Normans to protect their hunting. This was their stronghold.

6. Turn left and walk with a line of trees on the left. As you approach the Magna Carta Memorial bear right to a stile. Over the stile turn left to continue in the same direction past the monument and a path on the left leading to the Kennedy Memorial. Now head across to two lodges, the one on the left housing the teashop.

King John was a disaster as a monarch, levying heavy taxes to pay for unsuccessful foreign wars. He lost the support of the powerful, feudal barons, who rebelled against him in 1215. They forced him to sign a document granting them certain liberties and protection from injustice. The King was staying at Windsor and the rebellious barons were encamped at Staines so Runnymede was conveniently between the two with open space for tents and armies. The ordinary people got nothing from Magna Carta – they were beneath consideration – but the document embodied the principle that the law is above all and is the precursor of our democratic rights and freedoms.

> *'No free man shall be . . . imprisoned or . . . outlawed . . . except by the lawful judgement of his peers or by the law of the land. To no one will we sell, to no one will we deny or delay right or justice.'*

These principles were exported to the United States and the American Bar Association erected this memorial in 1957.

The Kennedy Memorial is on land given to the United States in memory of the assassinated President. Once through the gate you are technically on American soil. There is much symbolism in the design and setting, explained on a nearby board.

7. After tea cross the road to a path by the river and follow it downstream back to the start.

We don't know very much about what actually happened at the historic meeting between the barons and King John or where the Magna Carta was sealed; popular tradition says that it was on Magna Carta Island, which the route passes. The word 'Runnymede' means 'council island meadow'. After the reluctant King John had sealed the charter, copies were distributed throughout the land. Some alterations were subsequently made and the third and final version was confirmed by Edward I in 1297.

Walk 2
WINDSOR GREAT PARK

This interesting and varied walk straddles the Surrey – Berkshire border and is entirely within Windsor Great Park. It has much to recommend it – great views, attractive landscape, historical interest and a good tea. What more could you ask for? It is one of the longer walks in this book but the going is very easy, all on surfaced drives and clear paths and almost level. Before tea the route passes through Valley Garden (free admission), a delight at any time of year. It is well worth deviating from the suggested route to explore its nooks and crannies and you will certainly want to dawdle to enjoy this magical place so allow plenty of time.

 Savill Garden Restaurant looks out over another of the gardens within the park. It is housed in a modern building with floor to ceiling windows to make the most of its situation and there is also an extensive terrace with tables outside in the summer. A wide variety of excellent cakes is served together with other teatime goodies such as florentine biscuits and fruit pies and tarts. For lunch there is a tempting salad bar and jacket potatoes with a wide choice of fillings. There are other light savoury snacks including sandwiches and paté as well as a selection of hot meals. It is open throughout the year from 10 am until 6 pm. Telephone: 01784 432326.

DISTANCE: 7 miles.

MAP: OS Explorer 160 Windsor, Weybridge and Bracknell.

STARTING POINT: Bishopsgate entrance to Windsor Great Park (GR 978722).

HOW TO GET THERE: From the A328, the Old Windsor-Englefield Green road, ¾ mile south of its junction with the A308, take Castle Hill Road, signed 'Savill Court'. At a crossroads with Bishopsgate Road turn right and follow the road to its end at the Bishopsgate entrance to Windsor Great Park. There is free parking along the left of the road.

ALTERNATIVE STARTING POINT: If you wish to visit the teashop at the beginning or end of your walk, start at Savill Garden for which there is ample parking in the signed car park in Wick Lane, Englefield Green. You will then start the walk at point 11, turning left out of the teashop to begin the walk.

THE WALK

1. Go through the gate into the park and ahead on a surfaced drive for 50 yards. Fork right to walk with a deer fence on your right to meet a surfaced drive.

Deer roamed the Great Park for many centuries but were taken away in 1940 when many acres went under the plough as part of the war effort to increase food production. In 1979, at the suggestion of the Duke of Edinburgh, the present Chief Ranger, 1,000 acres were enclosed and the deer reintroduced.

2. Turn right through a gate into the deer park and follow the surfaced drive. Immediately after a short walled stretch leave the drive and bear left uphill to a statue.

This is Snow Hill. It is said that Henry VIII stood here awaiting news of the execution of Anne Boleyn, signalled by gunfire from the Tower of London. Mind you, he is also supposed to have been at several other places at the same time. The views from here are superb, especially down the Long Walk to Windsor Castle. The statue is of George III and was commissioned by his son, George IV. Sir Richard Westmacott created it between 1824 and 1830. Notice that the King has no stirrups. The story goes that the sculptor hanged himself when he realised he had forgotten them. As Sir Richard lived to a

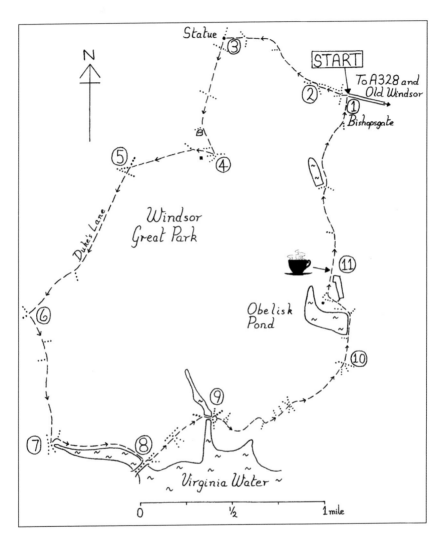

ripe old age, the story is not founded in truth. The statue was damaged
when the cart carrying it to Snow Hill broke. A furnace was set up on the
spot and repairs were made to the damaged leg.

3. Turn left on a grassy path. Leave the deer park through tall gates
and continue on the broad, grassy path, past a pond on the right,
to a complex junction of drives and tracks at Chaplain's Lodge.

Statue of George III on Snow Hill

4. Turn right. At a fork bear left on a narrower drive.

5. At a cross drive turn left. Follow Duke's Lane for nearly a mile, passing a drive on the left.

6. Just after a fence on the left ends, turn left on an unsurfaced, woodland track.

The Great Park is about 4,500 acres in all. A huge variety of trees thrive here and some of the oaks are over 500 years old. English elms more or less disappeared in the 20th century, ravaged by Dutch Elm disease. Careful management with replacement planting as and where necessary will ensure that it will be an outstandingly beautiful place for generations to come. It is said to be one of the best places to hear the dawn chorus in spring; not something that can be personally verified by the author!

7. When the track approaches a surfaced drive, turn left on a path signed 'No entry for horses'. Walk beside the ever-widening arm of a lake to a surfaced drive.

This lovely lake, which looks so natural, was created in the 18th century by damming the Virginia River. The instigator of this project was William, 1st Duke of Cumberland and the lake was designed by Thomas Sandby, landscape gardener and Deputy Ranger of the park from 1746 to 1789; some of his original plans are preserved in the library at Windsor Castle. The dam was completed and the lake filled by 1753 but during a violent storm 15 years later, the dam was washed away. It was repaired and the lake had reached its present form by 1790.

8. Turn left, soon picking up a walkers' path to the right of the drive and horse track. This eventually rejoins the drive. Turn right to cross another arm of the lake.

9. Take the second path on the right, signed 'Valley and Heather Gardens'. Turn left after 20 yards. When the path forks, bear right. Follow the clear main path through the gardens, ignoring many grassy paths to left and right unless you wish to explore these lovely gardens. The path leads down into a valley and up the other side to a complex junction of several surfaced paths. Continue ahead, signed 'Savill Garden and car park 1 mile'.

☕ **10.** At a surfaced cross drive carry on in the same direction, now on a surfaced drive, signed 'Savill Garden and car park ½ mile'. Pass the Obelisk Pond and obelisk to the teashop on the left at the entrance to Savill Garden.

The obelisk was raised by George II to mark the achievements of his son William, 1st Duke of Cumberland, who was appointed Ranger of Windsor Great Park after his victory over Bonnie Prince Charlie at Culloden in 1746.

Savill Garden, open all year from 10 am until 6 pm, or dusk if earlier, and for which there is a charge, was started in 1932 by Sir Eric Savill, the royal gardener. The flowering shrubs, such as rhododendrons and camellias, and herbaceous borders were laid out in 35 acres of woodland and were designed to provide colour all year round.

11. Turn left out of the teashop. When the main surfaced drive bends left, continue ahead to Bishopsgate entrance on the right, where this walk started.

Walk 3
CHOBHAM COMMON

Anyone interested in wildlife and landscape history will rate this an outstanding walk as it explores the largest National Nature Reserve in south-east England. It seems very wild and remote in parts, a long way from the wealthy and manicured image of the Home Counties. The outward route is mainly through woodland and then leaves the common to visit Chobham, an interesting and ancient place with an excellent traditional teashop. The return leg crosses the more open heathland and has splendid views across the common.

 Saddler's Halt in Chobham's High Street is a delightful teashop with an attractive wisteria-hung patio backed by an antique shop. The range of light lunches is excellent, including a tasty Chobham rarebit, smoked salmon with scrambled eggs or garlic mushrooms served with a savoury scone as well as the more usual sandwiches and filled jacket potatoes. A full roast lunch is served on Sunday. At teatime there are various set teas, including a cream tea, and, of course, tempting cakes are available all day. They are open every day between 9 am and 5 pm. Telephone: 01276 855808.

DISTANCE: 6 miles.

MAP: OS Explorer 160 Windsor, Weybridge and Bracknell.

STARTING POINT: Longcross car park (GR 979651).

HOW TO GET THERE: Longcross car park is on the B386 Chertsey-Windlesham road, about a mile east of the junction with the B383.

ALTERNATIVE STARTING POINT: If you wish to visit the teashop at the beginning or end of your walk, start in Chobham, where there is ample parking in the free car park on the High Street by Sadler's Halt. You will then start the walk at point 8.

THE WALK

1. Take a track at the rear of the car park for 200 yards, ignoring paths on the right, to an oblique cross path. Turn left. Follow the track, again ignoring paths on the right, to a T-junction with a similar track.

2. Turn left for 80 yards to another T-junction. Turn right. When the track forks after 50 yards, bear left. Pass under some pylons then, about 100 yards after the fork, turn right on a signed cross path.

About 150 years ago Chobham Common was part of a vast heathland covering 60% of north-west Surrey and large parts of neighbouring counties. It was a wild and remote area, notorious for highwaymen. Since then the growth in population and changes in agricultural methods have reduced it to a fragment of its former extent and lowland heath is one of the most threatened habitats in Britain. Chobham Common is an intricate mosaic of open heath, woodland and wet areas and is exceptionally rich in wildlife. It is nationally important for insects. Several butterflies and moths that are abundant here are uncommon elsewhere. The list of spiders is the longest in Britain and some of the species are very rare. One, which has no common English name, has not been recorded elsewhere in the UK. The ornithological interest is also outstanding with over 80 species recorded in recent years including the rare Dartford warbler and hobby. With such a long list of rare species and wide variety of habitats, it is not surprising that Chobham Common has been designated a Grade 1 Site of Special Scientific Interest and a National Nature Reserve.

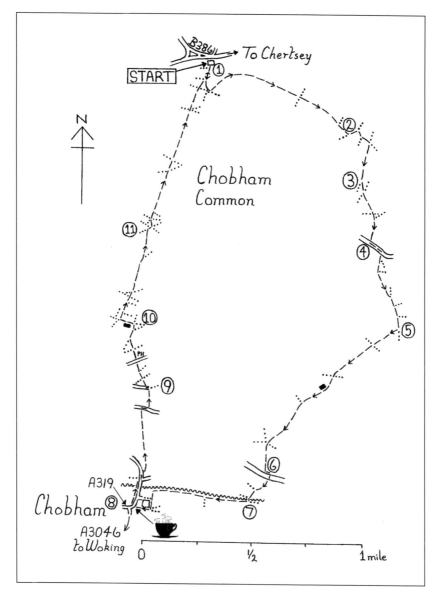

3. After about 350 yards watch for a smaller but clear path bearing left. Take this and go over an obvious cross path after 60 yards and continue ahead. Cross a second path and after a further 20 yards a major path joins on the left. Press on in the same direction to a lane.

4. Turn left for 140 yards then right on a signed bridleway along a track. After 30 yards, as the track bears left, go ahead on a signed path. Follow the path along the edge of a wood to a T-junction. Turn right along boards laid along the edge of a marshy area, and continue ahead, ignoring paths and a track on the left.

5. Watch for a stile on the right into a field. Go over this and walk along the left hand side of the first field and then right hand side of two small fields to a stile onto a track. Walk along the track, past farm buildings and carry on when the track becomes a surfaced drive to reach a main road.

6. Turn left for 40 yards then right on a signed path. After a few yards cross a stile then bear slightly right to a footbridge.

☕ 7. Cross the footbridge then turn right and follow a path beside the stream. The path eventually bears left away from the stream and leads into Chobham to emerge on the High Street next to the teashop.

In 1853 Queen Victoria reviewed the troops assembled on Chobham Common prior to their departure for the Crimea. The cannon on the small green in front of the teashop commemorates the visit. The original was loyally sent for scrap in 1942 to help the war effort but in 1979 the village was given a replacement on permanent loan from the National Artillery Museum.

8. From the teashop cross the road and turn right on a path beside the road but separated from it by a stream. When the path joins the main road continue in the same direction for 60 yards then bear right, signed 'Footpath no 49A', to eventually emerge in Burr Hill Lane. Turn right for 50 yards then left on a path next to house number 19. This path leads through to an unmade road. Walk along this until it turns sharp left and is surfaced.

9. Some 10 yards after the bend turn right on a signed path. After crossing a track it is called 'Red Lion Lane', even though it is just a footpath, but it soon becomes a track leading to the pub. Cross a road and continue on a track to the left of the pub. When this reaches a cross track press on in the same direction, now on a path a couple of yards to the right. This soon joins a path coming in from the left. Some 60 yards further on the track forks; bear left to a cross path after a further 40 yards.

10. Turn left for 100 yards, passing a large white building on the left, to a complex junction of several paths. Turn right and follow the broad path for a bare ½ mile to a large cross track.

The natural and timeless appearance of the heath is deceptive for this is a man-made landscape dating back to Neolithic times. Prehistoric farmers cleared the primeval forest from areas such as this, where the light sandy soils could easily be cultivated by primitive wooden ploughs. Robbed of the protective forest canopy the fragile soils deteriorated rapidly into vast tracts of impoverished acid soil, incapable of supporting agriculture. Grazing and the depredations of rabbits all helped to maintain the habitat as any tree seeds that managed to germinate were damaged by nibbling. This grazing pressure has declined with changes in agriculture and the effects of myxomatosis so the tree cover has increased. There are many young birches to be seen among the heather. Birch is a pioneer species. The trees don't live all that long – perhaps 100 years – but they alter the environment by allowing nutrients to accumulate in the soil paving the way for other species, such as oak, to colonise. Without management, the heath would eventually revert to the oak woodland from which it was formed with the loss of the unique wildlife that depends on it. The plan is to start grazing the common but that requires fencing, which needs special permission.

11. Turn right for 40 yards then left and follow the clear track across the heath, crossing several paths and tracks, to a T-junction. Turn left and retrace your steps back to the start. (Turn right here if you started in Chobham.)

Walk 4
BASINGSTOKE CANAL

The two parts of this walk make a pleasing and interesting contrast. The circuit starts and ends along the towpath of Basingstoke Canal, often described as Britain's most beautiful waterway. These stretches are linked by paths crossing pine-studded heath. The route calls in at Basingstoke Canal Centre with its informative displays and welcome tea room. There is also the chance for a short trip on the canal in the summer months and a visit to a floating art gallery.

The Canal Centre Tea Room at Mytchett offers a good selection of tempting and delicious home-made cakes, which may be supplemented with sandwiches and snacks for lunch. The interior is cheerful and there are also some tables outside overlooking the children's play area. They are open between 10.30 am and 4.30 pm every day except Monday from the beginning of April until the end of September. Telephone: 01252 370073.

When the teashop is closed, the canalside pub, the King's Head, passed soon after the start of the walk, serves food.

DISTANCE: 4½ miles.

MAP: OS Explorer 145 Guildford and Farnham.

STARTING POINT: Frimley Lodge Park, Frimley (GR 892560).

HOW TO GET THERE: From junction 4 of the M3 take the A331 south then the A325, signed 'Camberley Frimley'. Turn right at the first roundabout, signed 'Frimley Town Centre'. Turn left at a mini-roundabout. Follow the main road, bearing right at the junction with the B3012 on the B3411. Go under a railway bridge then turn left into Frimley Lodge Park. Bear right, signed 'Canal South Car Parks'. Bear left at a junction to the signed Car Park 2 by a miniature railway.

ALTERNATIVE STARTING POINT: If you wish to visit the teashop at the beginning or end of your walk, start at the car park for Basingstoke Canal Centre at Mytchett. The teashop is beyond the Canal Centre. You will then start the walk at point 8.

The Walk

Surrey Heath Council bought Frimley Lodge Park in 1983 to protect it from the threat of building development and to provide recreational open space. The 59 acre site was previously used as grazing land and the management plan tries to retain that character with grassy open spaces fringed with hedges and strips of deciduous woodland.

1. From the car park go ahead with the miniature railway on your right to the canal bank and turn left along the towpath. At a road bridge cross the canal and continue along the towpath on the other side. At the time of writing, the route is enlivened by some shop mannequins in a garden across the canal, dressed appropriately for the season. Continue under a bridge.

Two hundred years ago investment in canals was seen as the next big thing, rather like telecom shares at the end of the 20th century. Basingstoke Canal was planned to link the rich agricultural area of central Hampshire with London via the Thames. The 37 mile long canal included 29 locks, a 1,230 yard long tunnel, 69 bridges, five lock houses and four wharves and was constructed in six years; an impressive feat when you consider that the navvies had little more than pickaxes, wheelbarrows and shovels. It was opened on 4 September 1794 but was never a financial success because it was not part of a through route and faced increasing competition from improving roads and later the railways. Somehow, it managed to survive through the 19th century and was periodically revitalised to serve local developments. For example, the canal was used to carry materials for construction of the London to

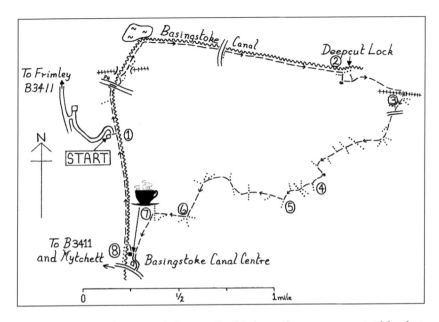

Southampton railway and then to build the military camp at Aldershot, started in 1854. Despite these temporary revivals, the story of the Basingstoke Canal through most of the 19th and 20th centuries is a slow decline into dereliction.

By the 1960s the canal was unnavigable. In some places it was completely dry and overgrown, in others it consisted of pools of water and at best was choked with weed and silt. The lock gates were rotting and the towpath was covered with vegetation. Its sad condition prompted a group of local canal enthusiasts to campaign for public ownership and restoration. Hampshire and Surrey County Councils bought the canal in 1976 and it has been restored by enthusiastic volunteer workers until now it is widely considered to be Britain's most beautiful inland waterway and is a Site of Special Scientific Interest, teeming with wildlife.

2. Just before a lock turn right on an unsigned path to shortly meet an unsurfaced drive and continue ahead. In front of a house follow this round to the left and press on when it becomes surfaced. Follow the drive through a gate and over the railway.

3. Some 30 yards after the bridge turn right on a path to a road. Cross the road and continue ahead, ignoring all side tracks, to a wooden shelter on the left.

4. About 100 yards after the shelter the track forks; bear right. Go over a major cross track and continue ahead for 150 yards.

This is part of the extensive Surrey heathland; see Walk 3 and Walk 13 for more details. Much of the heath close to the garrison towns of Aldershot and Farnborough has been given over to military use and the public are not welcome for obvious reasons. However, this corner is open to everyone and, though you may see groups in training, you are in no danger from unexploded ordnance.

5. Turn right. This is the second track on the right after the cross track, though the first is less obvious. Ignore a track branching left and join a track coming in from the left. After a further 40 yards bear left on a minor branch which merges with first one and then a second track coming in from the right.

6. At a major cross path, at a fence corner, turn right to continue beside the fence. When the major track bears left, continue ahead by the fence. Go over a cross path into a field.

 7. Turn left towards buildings, one of which is the teashop.

The Canal Centre has a wealth of information about the canal and also an exhibition about its history (telephone: 01252 370073). Boat trips on Daydream and Merlin start from here between Easter and September at the weekend and every day except Monday in the school holidays (telephone: 01252 378779). There is also a floating art gallery, Towed Haul, that displays the work of canal artist Nancy Larcombe.

8. From the teashop walk to the canal. Cross at a footbridge and turn right along the towpath back to the start. (Note: the footbridge may be closed when the Canal Centre is closed on Mondays. You may then reach the towpath on the far side of the canal by crossing at the road bridge beyond the Centre.)

The Basingstoke Canal has more species of aquatic plants, 102 in total, than any other waterway in Britain and is home to 25 species of dragonfly, two-thirds of the British total. Further west along the canal and not passed on this walk, the Greywell Tunnel is renowned as the largest winter bat roost in the country. The canal's unpolluted water supports a variety of fish including some specimens of carp over 30lb and pike of 27lb.

Walk 5
TILFORD AND THE RIVER WEY

This highly recommended route explores the lovely countryside round the confluence of one of Surrey's major rivers, the Wey. Starting at the well-known beauty spot of Frensham Little Pond, the route wends its way through woodland and beside the Wey to the ancient village of Tilford, a most picturesque place with an excellent riverside pub. More woodland walking leads to the Rural Life Centre with its welcoming café. This route can easily be made into a varied and interesting all-day expedition with lunch at the pub in Tilford, a visit to the museum and tea (spring, summer and autumn), followed by a short stroll back to the start.

 The Old Kiln Café at the Rural Life Centre has a cheerful interior and many tables outside under the trees. They serve an excellent range of tempting cakes or cream teas with clotted cream. For lunch possibilities include a choice of sandwiches and baguettes, filled jacket potatoes, salads and hot meals, including a roast on Sundays. You do not need to pay to go in the museum to visit the teashop, though a visit rounds out the day's expedition nicely; allow a couple of hours. The café is open between 11 am and 5 pm every day except Monday and Tuesday from April to the end of October. Telephone: 01252 794294.

When the teashop is closed the Barley Mow in Tilford serves good food and has a garden overlooking the river and an open fire in winter.

DISTANCE: 6 miles.

MAP: OS Explorer 145 Guildford and Farnham.

STARTING POINT: Frensham Common Little Pond car park (GR 856418).

HOW TO GET THERE: From the A287 Farnham-Hindhead road, about 3 miles south of Farnham, just beyond the Mariners Hotel, take a lane east, Priory Lane, signed 'Frensham Little Pond'. Follow it for ½ mile to the second, larger car park on the right.

ALTERNATIVE STARTING POINT: If you wish to visit the teashop at the beginning or end of your walk, start at the Rural Life Centre, where there is a car park. The teashop is by the entrance. Please seek permission before leaving a car for a long period. You will then start the walk at point 11. Turn left out of the Rural Life Centre along the road for 140 yards then bear left on a small path up to a track on a corner and turn right parallel with the road.

THE WALK

1. Return to the lane and turn right for 150 yards. Bear left along a track, continuing ahead at a building on the left.

2. Some 200 yards after a signed bridleway on the right, turn left over a stile on a signed, fenced footpath. Continue ahead as a track joins from the right at a farm.

3. When the track ahead is signed 'Private', fork left on a path waymarked by a yellow arrow on a post. This soon reaches the river Wey. Follow the path to a track and turn left to the road in Tilford.

This picturesque village has a long history, occupying an important position where two branches of the river Wey meet. The ancient bridges were originally built in the 13th century by monks from Waverley Abbey a mile away. The east bridge was restored in 1997 and a time capsule was planted between the fifth and sixth arches. A picture of the Spice Girls, a photograph of the Parish Council, a piece of Blu-Tack and a Teletubby were among the dozens of items placed to interest and amuse future generations. Tilford's glory is its immense village green, used as a cricket

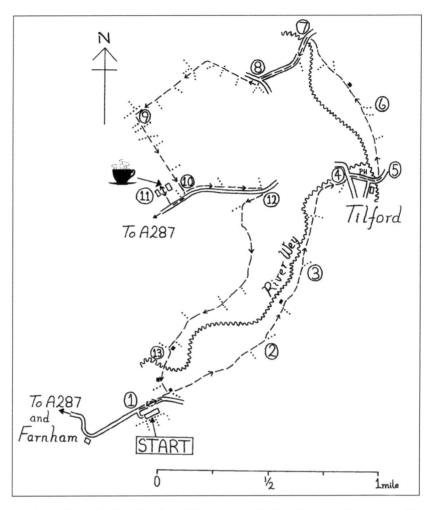

N

To A287

To A287
and
Farnham

Tilford

River Wey

START

0   ½   1 mile

pitch and overlooked by the 17th century Barley Mow and a venerable oak. Some say it is 'the oak at Kyngboc' mentioned in a charter dated 1128. This is disputed but it is at least 800 years old. The tree is now sadly reduced and patched up now, not at all 'the finest tree I ever saw in my life' described by William Cobbett, writing in the 19th century.

4. Head across the corner of the village green to the ancient oak and turn right along a road, passing the Barley Mow on the left. Continue along the road, signed for Elstead, Milford and Godalming, crossing a bridge over the river.

5. Some 30 yards after the bridge turn left on a signed bridleway and follow it to a surfaced drive.

6. Turn left. Continue ahead when the drive becomes a path after Tilhill House, forking left after a further 200 yards. Press on in the same direction at the next junction to reach a lane.

7. Turn left and walk along the lane to a T-junction with a road.

8. Take a signed bridleway opposite the junction. Turn right along a cross path after 20 yards to walk parallel with the road. Ignore paths on the left and then follow the main path as it bears round to the left and continue ahead along a broad, grassy ride.

9. At the end of the ride turn left along another broad ride, first going uphill and then down again. Ignore numerous paths to left and right.

☕ **10.** When the ride ends * note this point and bear right to the road and turn right along it for 140 yards to the Rural Life Centre on the right. The teashop is by the entrance.

Madge and Henry Jackson founded the Rural Life Centre in 1973. It now occupies ten acres and has more than 40,000 artefacts reflecting the dramatic changes in rural life in the last two hundred years. There are several reconstructed buildings and craftsmen regularly demonstrate their skills. It is open from April to October, Wednesday to Sunday and Bank Holiday Mondays, 11 am until 6 pm; and on Wednesdays in winter, 11 am to 4 pm. Telephone: 01252 795571.

11. Retrace your steps to the point * noted before but now continue parallel with the road to a T-junction. Turn right to rejoin the road.

12. Cross the road to a bridleway opposite. Carry on when the track becomes a path and follow it for about ¾ mile to a farm, ignoring all side turns.

13. Bear left past the farm buildings and follow the path over the river Wey. At a fork just after Keepers Cottage bear left to the building passed soon after the start of the walk. Turn right and retrace your steps back to the start. (If you started at the Rural Life Centre or in Tilford turn left here.)

Walk 6
GIBBET HILL AND THE DEVIL'S PUNCH BOWL

The only difficulty with this excellent walk is deciding when to do it. The Devil's Punch Bowl is an amazing geological feature and is part of Hindhead Common, owned by the National Trust. In late summer the heather is a purple, scented sea. In spring the gorse is covered in vibrant golden blossom and the many species of tree are just coming into leaf, always a delight. The autumn colours make a blazing show and in winter the superb views are at their best. I suggest that the solution to this conundrum is to do the walk several times and make up your own mind! Whenever you decide, make sure it is a clear day to enjoy this route's very best feature – the outstanding views.

 The Devil's Punch Bowl Café is run by the National Trust and offers the usual excellent fare that we have come to expect from this organisation. There is a selection of delicious cakes and, for lunch, sandwiches and a choice of daily specials. Some seats outside complement the airy and modern interior. They are open every day between 8 am and 5 pm, perhaps closing earlier in the depths of winter. Telephone: 01428 608771.

DISTANCE: 4 miles.
MAP: OS Explorer 133 Haslemere and Petersfield.
STARTING POINT: Boundless Copse (GR 901370).
HOW TO GET THERE: From the A3 between Guildford and Petersfield, about 2 miles north of Hindhead, take a lane signed 'Brook'. The junction is at the point where the A3 changes from single carriageway to dual carriageway (going north). Drive along the lane for ½ mile to a track on the right leading into Boundless Copse, recognisable by the Forest Enterprise sign and the drive to Begley Farm on the left. There is parking for several cars.
ALTERNATIVE STARTING POINT: If you wish to visit the teashop at the beginning or end of your walk, start in the National Trust Hindhead Common car park, near the junction of the A3 and A287. There is a charge for parking here and it can be very busy. The teashop is at the rear of the car park. You will then start the walk at point 5.

THE WALK
1. Facing the lane turn right along it for ¼ mile.

2. Immediately before the drive to The Lodge at Boundless Farm turn right uphill on a signed public footpath along a forestry track. Ignore a track on the left after 100 yards. When the track forks after a further 100 yards, bear left to continue uphill. After a cross path, the way narrows but press on uphill.

3. When the path levels out, bear left at a fork, waymarked as a National Trust path. After a further 50 yards cross a bridleway and continue ahead, now waymarked as the Greensand Way, to the top of Gibbet Hill, marked by a Celtic cross and trig point. To the left are some seats well placed to enjoy the spectacular view.

At 895 feet this is the second highest point in Surrey (Leith Hill – see Walk 16 – is the highest) and the third highest in south-east England. The views used to be even more spectacular but trees have restricted all but the easterly vista in recent years. To the east you can see to Kent on a clear day and Hydon's Ball (see Walk 8) is a prominent feature. The main London-Portsmouth road used to come right over the hill until the advent of motor

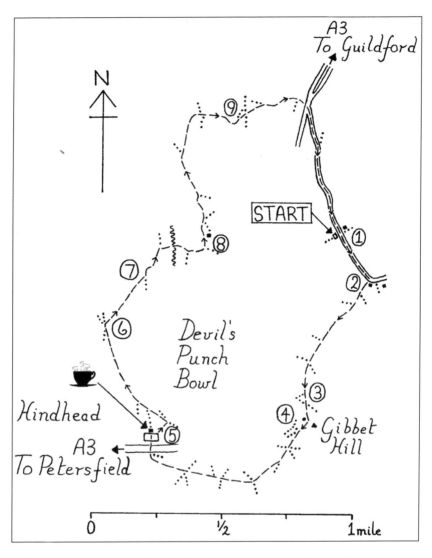

N↑

A3
To Guildford

⑨

START

①

②

⑧

⑦

⑥

Devil's
Punch
Bowl

③

④ Gibbet
Hill

⑤

Hindhead

A3
To Petersfield

| 0 | ½ | 1 mile |

vehicles meant its route had to be changed to ease the gradient. In 1787 three men were hanged on the spot where the cross now stands for a particularly sordid murder. A sailor, whose name was never discovered, was walking to Portsmouth to rejoin his ship or seek a new one. He fell in with three other men at a pub near Godalming and paid their bill, as they had no money. The next day all four journeyed on together and stopped at the Red Lion in Thursley. Here he treated them again. They repaid his

The cross on Gibbet Hill

generosity by brutally stabbing him to death and stripping his body, which they abandoned in the Devil's Punch Bowl. It was soon discovered and the villains were caught at Rake, near Petersfield, trying to sell their victim's clothes. They were tried, convicted and hanged in chains. Their bodies were left hanging from the 30 foot gibbet for years afterwards, as a warning to travellers. The sailor was buried in Thursley. His sad epitaph contains these lines:

> *'In perfect Health and in the Flower of Age*
> *I fell a Victim to three Ruffians' Rage'.*

☕ **4.** With your back to the seats, go ahead on a broad, grassy path. Continue ahead on a National Trust path at a disused parking area, ignoring paths bearing right. Cross a track and, after a further 130 yards, bear right, still waymarked as the Greensand Way. At a junction with a sandy track press on in the same direction and follow the track to the A3 and the teashop across the road at the rear of the car park.

5. Take a path from the right rear of the car park. This leads to the rim of the Devil's Punch Bowl with outstanding views across it. Turn left along the upper path, signed 'Highcombe Edge'. Follow this to a track junction at an electricity sub-station.

This vast natural amphitheatre is Surrey's most celebrated natural feature. The steep sides drop 350 feet to Highcomb Bottom. The Saxons called it Wolves Den and the present name first appears on a map published in 1775 so it is probably just a bit of whimsy from the start of the tourist industry. Punch bowl is quite apt, however. Sometimes, morning mist lying in the bowl rises and flows over the edge so it looks as if it is boiling.

6. Turn immediately right, not along the track to Broom Acres. After a few yards turn right downhill on a signed bridleway. Follow this steeply down into the valley to meet a cross path.

7. Turn left for about 250 yards then right through wooden gates to carry on downhill on a sunken track. Cross a footbridge and carry on up the other side to a broad cross track. Turn left.

It is hard to credit that this natural chasm has been eroded over thousands of years by the springs that rise higher up and form this stream. The Devil's Punch Bowl is one of the largest spring-eroded valleys in Europe.

8. Go through gates across the track onto a section of surfaced track. Turn left again. Follow this track, passing the quaintly named 'Gnome Cottage', for just over ½ mile.

The cottages scattered about the valley bottom were once inhabited by 'broom squires', families who made a living producing brooms. With the busy London–Portsmouth road with its rich traffic so close by, they were not averse to other, less honourable ways of making a living.

9. When the track forks, bear right. Shortly cross another track and continue ahead to the A3. Cross this extremely busy and noisy road to the lane opposite and walk along it back to the start.

Walk 7
BLACK DOWN AND HASLEMERE

This superb walk straddles the Surrey/Sussex border. It visits the highest point in Sussex, Black Down, but is included because the teashop and most of the route are in Surrey. It is one of the longer walks in this book and there is a steady climb from Haslemere to Black Down but the stupendous views and outstanding woodland walking are worth every ounce of effort. Haslemere is an attractive small town, home to an excellent teashop, giving sustenance to tackle the more demanding second leg.

Although named 'coffee shop', Darnleys is also a traditional teashop very popular with the people of Haslemere. It serves an excellent range of delicious cakes and other teatime goodies including cream teas with clotted cream. The range of sandwiches is similarly excellent, and if you are hungrier there is a selection of hot daily specials. As well as the attractive interior, there are also some tables outside overlooking the broad High Street. They are open between 9.15 am and 5 pm every day except Sunday. In summer they open on Sunday as well between 10.30 am and 4 pm. Telephone: 01428 643048. When the teashop is closed there are several pubs in Haslemere that serve food.

DISTANCE: 7½ miles.
MAP: OS Explorer 133 Haslemere and Petersfield.
STARTING POINT: Black Down car park (GR 920308). If this is full, there is another car park down the track to the left.
HOW TO GET THERE: From the B2131 at the eastern edge of Haslemere take a minor road, Haste Hill, signed for Black Down and Whitwell Hatch. At crossroads after ¼ mile go straight ahead on Tennyson's Lane, signed 'Black Down'. Take the first left, to continue on Tennyson's Lane, for a mile to a car park on the right.
ALTERNATIVE STARTING POINT: If you wish to visit the teashop at the beginning or end of your walk, start in Haslemere where there is ample parking in a signed car park (fee) behind the High Street. The teashop is on the High Street. You will then start the walk at point 9.

THE WALK

1. Facing the road take a narrow path on the right hand side of the car park, passing a National Trust notice board, to a T-junction with a track. Turn right. At a fork bear left along a somewhat narrower track, shortly joining a track coming in from the right. Continue ahead, bearing left when the track forks again.

Objects found on Black Down suggest the area was settled as long ago as 6000 BC. Early farmers favoured such areas because the thin forest cover was easy to clear. However, the thin soil quickly became impoverished and heath developed, fit only for rough grazing. Changes in farming have led to a decline in grazing and self-sown pines have invaded. Heath is a rare and threatened habitat in Southern England: it is estimated perhaps half has been lost since the middle of the 20th century. Therefore the management policy for Black Down is to increase the amount of heath by cutting it to simulate grazing and weeding out trees. Trees on the slopes were never cleared in the same way as the ground is too steep for farming. The slopes are mainly clothed in ancient beech woodland that supports nationally rare species, such as the splendidly named flat-footed fly.

2. When the main track bends right about a mile from the car park, bear left, waymarked as a National Trust path. This leads to the Temple of the Winds. After admiring the view, retrace your steps to the main track and turn left along it. Bear right at the next junction

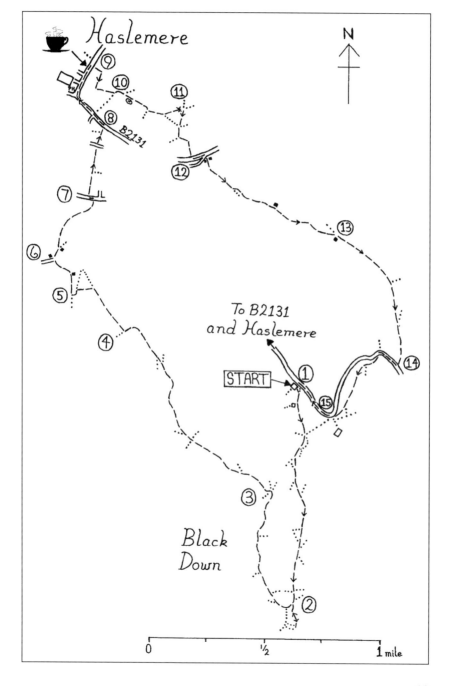

after 45 yards. When the track forks again by a seat after a further 150 yards, bear right to contour round the hill, passing more seats and another view plaque to a complex junction of paths and tracks.

The somewhat fancifully named Temple of the Winds is a superb viewpoint with a welcome seat that commemorates the gift of Black Down to the National Trust in 1944 by W.E. Hunter in memory of his wife.

3. Take a track on the left for 260 yards (not the path sharp left) then bear left at a fork, signed 'Sussex Border Path 1989'. Continue ahead at a cross path then, when the track forks after a further 80 yards, bear right. Now watch for a less obvious fork, waymarked by yellow arrows on a short, wooden post: bear left then continue ahead as a path joins on the right after 50 yards.

4. Some 40 yards after passing through a gate and leaving the wood, turn right across a field. Go through a second gate and turn left downhill. At the bottom of the field turn left through a gate and follow the track to a surfaced drive.

5. Turn right. Pass Valewood Farm House.

6. In front of the next house, Stedlands Farm, turn right along a gravelled track. When this ends by another house, continue ahead on a path, forking left after 10 yards. Follow this up to a road.

7. Turn left for 30 yards then right on a surfaced path. Cross a road and continue on the path, now down steps, to another road.

8. Turn left into Haslemere. Turn right along the High Street to the teashop on the left.

Haslemere has very old foundations. A weekly market and annual fair, confirmed in a charter from Richard II in 1394, was held in front of the Town Hall. The fair was revived in 1982 and is held every other year on the first Bank Holiday in May. Many artists and scientists chose to live in this attractive place. Among them was the eminent 19th century scientist, John Tyndall. He suffered from insomnia as he grew older and one night in December 1893 his devoted wife made a terrible mistake and gave him a lethal dose of his sleeping draught. He realised what had happened and his last words are among the saddest ever spoken, 'Darling, you have killed your John.'

9. Turn left out of the teashop then right along Well Lane. This shortly becomes a path that leads to the right, passing the old town well. Go through a gate on the left and across a field to a track.

Haslemere Educational Museum is just beyond Well Lane on the High Street. It started as the private collection of another eminent Victorian living in Haslemere, the surgeon Sir Jonathon Hutchinson. He opened his life's collection to the public in 1888 and supplemented this by Sunday afternoon lectures and demonstrations. It moved to its present premises in a handsome Queen Anne house on the High Street in 1926 and the galleries were substantially refurbished in 2002. It is well worth a visit. Admission is free and the museum is open from Tuesday to Saturday, 10 am to 5 pm. Telephone: 01428 642112.

10. Turn left. When the track bends right, continue on a signed path across a field. Bear left across a second field.

11. Cross a footbridge then turn right and follow the path across a muddy track. Bear left at the end of a field on the left and follow the path to a road.

12. Turn left for 70 yards. Immediately after a road on the right take a surfaced drive between a half-timbered house called Courts and Courts Cottage. Walk along the drive: the 'private' sign refers to vehicles, not people. Bear left at the entrance gates to Lythe Hill Estate. After stables on the left the track becomes a path; press on in the same direction. When the path leaves the wood, continue across a field to meet a track at High Barn Farm.

13. Turn right. The track shortly becomes a less distinct path but is easy enough to follow and eventually joins a track. Walk along the track to a lane.

14. Turn right. Some 10 yards after the entrance to 'Owlden' turn left on a National Trust path. Bear right when the path forks and follow the narrow but clear path uphill. Soon after the path levels out, fork right when the main path bears left. This branch leads to the lane at its junction with two tracks. (If you miss this point and reach a track, turn right to the lane.)

15. Turn left along the lane back to the start.

Walk 8
HYDON'S BALL AND WINKWORTH ARBORETUM

This walk in the woods includes a visit to the National Trust's only arboretum. Much of the woodland on the greensand ridge running across this part of Surrey is owned by the National Trust and this charming short walk explores one corner. It starts with a climb to the top of Hydon's Ball, a fine viewpoint with extensive vistas south and west. The climb can be omitted if you wish, though it amply rewards the small extra effort involved. The rest of the route is more level and all on clear paths and tracks. It wends its way through the woods to Winkworth Arboretum for tea and is short enough to combine with a visit, particularly recommended at bluebell time and in the autumn. The return leg through the pine-scented woods of Juniper Valley is sheer delight.

 The splendid National Trust tea room at Winkworth Arboretum is housed along with a small shop in a modern building next to the entrance. They serve a selection of home-made cakes including, on my visit, an unusual and tasty marmalade and fruit cake. For a light lunch there are delicious filled rolls, a ploughman's or quiche and salad. You will find a handful of tables inside and plenty of accommodation outdoors in a particularly attractive woodland setting. The tea room is open every day except Monday and Tuesday from late March until mid November, 11 am until 5 pm or dusk. It is also open every day when the bluebells and autumn colours are at their best and on Bank Holiday Mondays. During the winter it is open at weekends but closes completely between mid December and mid January. Telephone: 01483 208265.

DISTANCE: 4½ miles.

MAP: OS Explorer 145 Guildford and Farnham and 133 Haslemere and Petersfield.

STARTING POINT: Hydon's Ball car park (GR 979402).

HOW TO GET THERE: Take the B2130 Godalming-Hascombe road. About a mile south of Godalming town centre, at the edge of the built-up area, turn westwards on Home Farm Road, signed 'Milford H'bledon' for about 200 yards then left on Hambledon Road for about a mile. Turn left along Clock Barn Lane, signed 'West Surrey Cheshire Home Hydon Heath'. At a T-junction, signed 'Hascombe Dunsford' to the left and 'Hambledon Milford' to the right, go more or less straight on, slightly left, along a track. There is no car park sign but you pass the National Trust sign for Hydon's Ball. The entrance to the car park is on the left after 50 yards.

ALTERNATIVE STARTING POINT: If you wish to visit the teashop at the beginning or end of your walk, there is a car park at Winkworth Arboretum but this is only available to National Trust members or those visiting the Arboretum. The teashop is behind the car park. You will then start the walk at point 10.

THE WALK

1. Return to the track leading to the car park and turn left. Go over a cross path and continue ahead for 120 yards. (Note: if you do not wish to visit the viewpoint, continue along the track to rejoin the route at point 4.)

2. Watch for several water company posts on the right at a path junction. Bear half right uphill then right again when the path forks and follow the path to the top of the hill.

The hill contains an underground reservoir, hence the numerous manhole covers and vents.

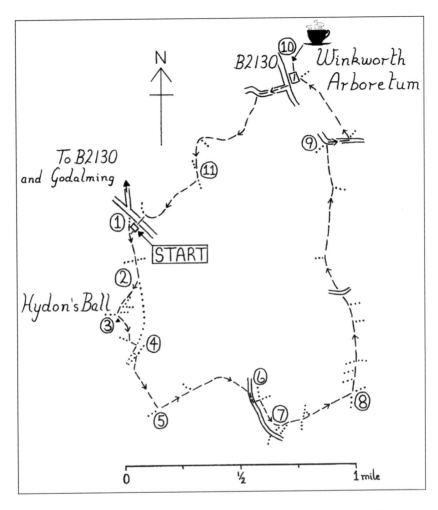

3. Leave the hilltop by the path to the left of the stone column, a trig point for Ordnance Survey mapping. Join a path coming in from the right and follow it down to rejoin the track.

4. Turn right for 50 yards then turn left to a T-junction with a cross path after 25 yards. Turn right and follow the sandy path initially along the edge of the wood with a fence on the left and then between fields to a T-junction with a track.

5. Turn left and walk along the track to a road.

6. Turn right for 120 yards then take a path on the left. After 10 yards turn right to walk parallel with the road for about 250 yards to a T-junction with a path.

7. Turn left and walk up through a wood. Go over an oblique cross path as the path levels out and continue ahead for about ¼ mile to an obvious cross path waymarked by blue arrows on a post.

8. Turn left. Ignore all side turns and continue ahead across a tiny lane. The track eventually becomes a surfaced drive. Press on ahead when another surfaced drive joins from the right to a road.

9. Turn right for 190 yards. Just before a steep hill sign turn left on a signed path that leaves the road at the same point as the drive to Eden House. This leads to the car park for Winkworth Arboretum. Turn right through the car park and right again to the tea room by the entrance.

Winkworth Arboretum was the creation of one man, Dr Wilfred Fox who lived at the nearby Winkworth Farm. At the time his extravagant and exotic planting was criticised as a blot on the landscape, but it is difficult to argue with his vision today now it has come to maturity in spectacular displays of spring and autumn colour. The Arboretum is open throughout the year during daylight hours. Telephone: 01483 208477.

10. Return to the car park and walk across to the far left corner. Cross the road and take South Munstead Lane opposite. When the lane bends right, turn left along a track. When the track ends continue ahead on a path that eventually leads down into Juniper Valley. Note: the path dips down before you reach the bottom of the valley. Keep going until you reach the bottom and meet a path coming in from the right.

11. Turn left on the path along the valley bottom. When this forks after 55 yards bear right and climb up out of the valley. Just before the path takes a sharp turn to the right, take a short path on the left to a stile onto a road. Cross the road and follow an unsigned path through the wood to return to the car park where this walk started.

Walk 9
LOSELEY PARK AND THE NORTH DOWNS WAY

This undemanding short walk through charming countryside is ideal for a saunter on a summer's afternoon or a brisk pipe opener in winter. The outward leg is through the well-kept pastures of Loseley Park, quintessentially English landscape. After refreshment for the body at an outstanding teashop, and for the mind at an art gallery devoted to an eminent Victorian artist, the return is mainly through woodland along the North Downs Way, which here follows the line of an ancient pilgrims' route. In such a tranquil, rural setting it is hard to believe you are just on the outskirts of Guildford.

The Teashop at Watts Gallery near Compton is a delightful traditional country tea room with a very tempting selection of cakes. All scones, jams and cakes are made on the premises using free range eggs and traditional methods, and you are sometimes able to buy cakes to take home with you too. Choices for lunch include things on toast such as a very tasty rarebit, sandwiches and a daily special. There is an exceptionally wide selection of teas available and these are also for sale in the small shop. There are some tables outside. The Teashop is open between 10.30 am and 5.30 pm every day except over Christmas and New Year. Telephone: 01483 811030. There is no other source of refreshment on this walk.

DISTANCE: 3½ miles.
MAP: OS Explorer 145 Guildford and Farnham.
STARTING POINT: Pilgrims' Way south of Guildford (GR 977479).
HOW TO GET THERE: From the A3100 Guildford-Godalming road, a mile south of Guildford, take a lane to the west called Sandy Lane. This is opposite Ye Olde Shippe Inn. Follow this for a mile to a very sharp left hand bend. On the bend turn right on a track where there are several parking spots, especially just along a track shortly on the left.
ALTERNATIVE STARTING POINT: If you wish to visit the teashop at the beginning or end of your walk, there is some limited roadside parking near Watts Gallery or the teashop has a car park, though permission should be sought before leaving a car for a lengthy period. You will then start the walk at point 6.

THE WALK

1. Return to the lane and continue ahead, now downhill on Littleton Lane, for about ¼ mile.

2. Take a signed path on the right at a phone box. This starts along a track and then is obvious on the ground across three fields to pass a small lake. At the end of the lake press on in the same direction, along the left hand side of the next field, to a track. Cross the track and continue round the left hand perimeter of the next field to a stile on the left. Cross the stile and carry on in the same direction to another track.

Loseley House, across the lake, is a fine example of Elizabethan architecture, built in 1562 by Sir William More. His masons found a ready source of worked stone at nearby Waverley Abbey and so his new house was mellow even as it was constructed. Elizabeth I slept here, as everywhere else. A letter from Lord Burghley in the family records warns Sir Christopher More that the entertainment had better be up to standard. On the whole, the More family stayed out of the turbulent mainstream of history, farming their rich acres. There are no periods languishing in jail, no sequestrations or executions. The most exciting occurrence was when Anne More secretly married John Donne and her furious father had the

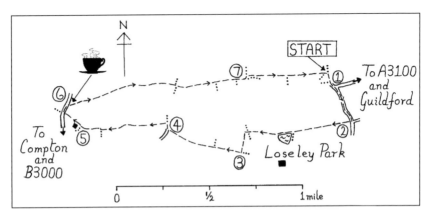

poet thrown in Fleet prison. The family still occupy Loseley Park, but the Loseley name is probably more famous now because of its dairy products.

3. Turn right along the track.

4. The track reaches a junction of surfaced drives, a lane and a path. Turn right on a signed bridleway for 50 yards then turn left up some steps and follow the initially fenced path to a cross path. Turn right to a track then left along the track to continue in the same direction.

5. As the track approaches a large barn, bear right over a stile, not through a metal field gate. This path leads to a road. Turn right to the teashop and Watts Gallery.

George Frederick Watts, born in 1817, was a largely self-taught artist. In 1886 he married his second wife, Mary Fraser-Tyler, also an artist and 33 years his junior. They came to the country to avoid the fogs in London and liked rural Surrey so much they decided to build a house here. Mrs Watts was firmly convinced of her husband's genius and the idea of a gallery to display his works was conceived. A friend, Christopher Turnor, designed the gallery, and Watts himself laid the foundation stone a few months before he died. The gallery is open free to the public in the afternoons. Mrs Watts also designed a truly extraordinary mortuary chapel for the village cemetery on the outskirts of Compton, down the lane. It looms over the village in bright red brick and terracotta and the inside is decorated in extravagant Art Nouveau style, heavy with symbolism.

The lake at Loseley Park

6. Return to the lane and turn left then immediately left again along a sandy track, the North Downs Way (or you can cut through to the track just before the road). Continue ahead at a cross track despite the notices: they refer to the woods on either side, not the track.

The high ground to the left is the Hog's Back. It now carries the A31 but has been an important route since the end of the last Ice Age. Prehistoric routes were often along the tops of ridges to avoid thick forest and marsh in the valleys below. Later, when there were fewer dangers from wolves and other wild animals in the woods, routes tended to move off the ridges and this track is probably one such. It is sometimes referred to as the Pilgrims' Way. In fact, there appears to be scant reference to this before the 1860s when someone at the Ordnance Survey presumably thought it sounded appropriate. Of course, Chaucer's famous pilgrims travelled from London to Canterbury and so probably followed the line of the A2 but travellers would have come this way from the ancient secular capital at Winchester to England's spiritual centre at Canterbury. Many of these ancient paths have been combined into the North Downs Way from Farnham to Dover, officially opened in 1978 following 15 years of planning and negotiation.

7. The track bends left. Ignore a path on the right at the bend and continue ahead for 20 yards to a track junction. Turn right and this track leads back to the start.

Walk 10
ST MARTHA'S HILL AND NEWLANDS CORNER

This is a glorious walk in one of the best-loved corners of Surrey. It starts by traversing St Martha's Hill, crowned with an ancient Norman church, then climbs again to Newlands Corner so it is quite an energetic hike. Newlands Corner is deservedly popular as perhaps the outstanding viewpoint in the county. It is served by a lively teashop with a garden facing the famous vista. The route returns through woodland studded with immensely old yews before more magnificent views will tempt you to linger on the hillside. There is little road walking and the paths are mainly dry and well made, making this a highly recommended circuit for all seasons.

 The New Barn Coffee Shop is modern and purpose built. It is very popular with the diverse visitors to this beauty spot. Cream teas include proper clotted cream with a reduced rate for two! For lunch there is a good choice of filled baguettes or jacket potatoes or complete meals if you are really hungry. A full English breakfast is served all day. This is complemented by tempting teatime treats such as millionaire's shortcake and flapjacks, with or without raisins. There is an extensive garden and patio. They are open every day throughout the year from 8 am until 5 pm and later in the summer. Telephone: 01483 222820.

DISTANCE: 4 miles.
MAP: OS Explorer 145 Guildford and Farnham.
STARTING POINT: Halfpenny Lane car park at St Martha's Hill (GR 022484).
HOW TO GET THERE: From the A248 Godalming-Shere road, at Chilworth take a minor road called Blacksmith Lane, signed 'St Martha Tyting'. Continue when it becomes Halfpenny Lane for about a mile from the A248 to a car park on the right. At the time of writing, there is no sign for the car park from this direction.
ALTERNATIVE STARTING POINT: If you wish to visit the teashop at the beginning or end of your walk, start at Newlands Corner on the A25 where there is a large car park. The teashop is across the road. You will then start the walk at point 5.

THE WALK

1. Leave the right rear of the car park to pick up a drive. Turn left then bear left after a few yards along a broad, sandy track, the North Downs Way. Follow the main track to the top of the hill, crowned by St Martha's church. Pass to the left of the church and press on in the same direction, now downhill and shortly passing a pillbox and information board.

Sitting on the summit of a hill 573 feet above sea level, the site of St Martha's has been a place of worship since the Bronze Age. It is the only church in England that is dedicated to St Martha, the sister of St Mary Magdalene and tradition says that she visited this spot when travelling with Lazarus and St Joseph of Arimathea. By the 19th century the church had fallen into disrepair but was skilfully restored. No attempt was made to reconstruct the original but the building remains true to the Norman spirit. At the bottom of the hill lies Chilworth village, home to a major gunpowder works from the early 17th century until 1920. It was so important that a Zeppelin raider sought it out during World War I but only managed to kill a swan.

2. At a three-way fork bear left towards a car park then turn right beside it. Continue in the same direction along a path to shortly

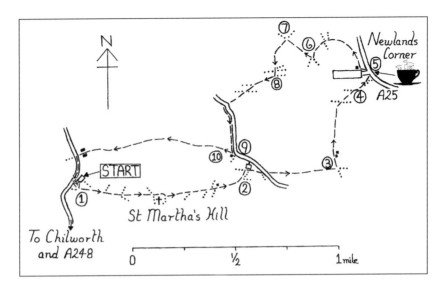

reach a lane. Take a fenced bridleway on the opposite side of the lane to a cross path.

3. Turn left, passing a farmhouse and barn. Continue in the same direction up a field to a wooden kissing gate. Bear slightly right over a second field, crossing one major cross path to a second cross path.

4. Turn right. As you approach a car park bear right to a road and the teashop on the other side.

In 1926 Newlands Corner was the site of a massive public search. Agatha Christie was already famous as an author of detective stories but her marriage was in difficulties. On 4th December she disappeared from home and her car was found at Newlands Corner. On Sunday 12th December a mass search for clues as to her fate was organised. She turned up a couple of days later at a hotel in Harrogate. She would never speak about what happened and whether her disappearance was a publicity stunt, a cry for help or a mental breakdown remains a matter of conjecture.

5. Recross the road and go into the car park. Take a path on the right leading past some public toilets. Follow the main path for about ¼ mile then watch for an interestingly designed seat on the right.

St Martha's church

6. Turn right here and take the path to the right of the seat. Follow this path to an obvious cross path.

7. Turn left and follow the broad, main path to meet a cross path at the top of a slope. Go ahead across this for 50 yards to a grassy cross path at the edge of the wood.

8. Turn right. When you reach a fork marked by a yellow waymark, bear left, signed 'North Downs Way'. Follow this down through more woods to a lane. Cross the lane and go up a few steps to continue on the North Downs Way, now parallel with the lane.

9. The path eventually reaches a cross track in front of a cottage. Turn right (the left branch leads to the lane). Walk along the track, eventually passing between farm buildings, to a lane.

10. Turn left back to the car park where this walk started.

Walk 11
GOMSHALL AND SHERE

This interesting and varied walk typifies the best that Surrey has to offer. Starting at one attractive village, it climbs the North Downs then follows an ancient drove road through woodland before dropping down to the neighbouring community of Shere. This is often described as one of the prettiest villages in Surrey. It has a wealth of fine buildings, one of which houses an excellent traditional teashop. The return is an easy stroll on a good path and, due to the tree-covered aspect of the North Downs hereabouts, it has the better views.

As a young man, the architect Edwin Lutyens courted the daughter of the local Lord of the Manor, Helen (known as Nellie) Bray. Sadly for him, she chose another suitor. Her father, perhaps to console the luckless Edwin, gave him several local commissions and the building that now houses the Lucky Duck was the first of these. It was originally a barber's shop and shoe shop but now houses a fine teashop with the added attraction of an immaculately maintained garden at the back. For lunch there is a good choice of light meals such as chicken and mushroom crêpes, coronation chicken, a ploughman's or a well thought out selection of sandwiches, served with a substantial salad and crisps. A splendid selection of cakes is served and as an alternative there are delicious desserts on offer, such as treacle tart or bannoffee pie. The traditional teatime treats including a cream tea will also tempt you. They are open every day throughout the year between 9 am and 5 pm, closing a little later in the summer. Telephone: 01483 202445.

DISTANCE: 4½ miles.
MAP: OS Explorer 145 Guildford and Farnham.
STARTING POINT: Gomshall Station car park (GR 089478).
HOW TO GET THERE: Gomshall is on the A25 between Guildford and Dorking, about 6 miles west of Dorking. The station is signed from the road.
ALTERNATIVE STARTING POINT: If you wish to visit the teashop at the beginning or end of your walk, start in Shere where there is limited street parking but usually space in the recreation ground car park behind the village hall. The teashop is in the centre of the village on Middle Street. You will then start the walk at point 7.

THE WALK

1. From the car park cross the railway and take a path from the platform that leads down to the A25.

2. Turn left, crossing the road to use the footway on the opposite side to walk out of the village.

3. Just after the entrance to Tillingbourne Trout Farm on the right, turn left along a track. Follow the track under the railway and uphill for about ¾ mile, ignoring all paths to the right and left, to a small clearing.

4. Turn left, signed 'North Downs Way'. Follow the waymarked path to an obvious cross path with an information board and a welcome seat.

5. Turn left for 50 yards, still on the North Downs Way, to a second cross track and turn left again. Continue along the main track, passing a curious round structure, for a good mile to reach a second, similar structure at an obvious cross path.

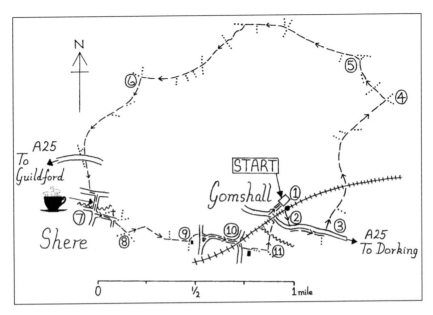

This bridleway is an old drove road or packhorse track along the top of the North Downs. Its origins go back into the mists of prehistoric times when it offered a high level route to the sea at Dover. Many ancient routes used the chalk uplands of Southern England. Chalk drains freely and was covered by light woodland so the going was easy, dry and level whereas the Weald below had wet clay covered with thick forest, the home of dangerous wild animals.

☕ **6.** Turn left. Follow the track downhill *, through a tunnel under the A25, to the road in Shere. Turn left, then right along Middle Street to the teashop on the right.

* Note the pillbox on your left as you descend the hill, one of several built during the Second World War to guard the southern approaches to London when the country was under threat of invasion. It is now surrounded by trees and would not be much use as a lookout but when it was built it commanded wide views across the valley. This shows just how much the countryside can change in as little as sixty years.

7. Turn right out of the teashop then take the first on the left, passing the church. At Church Hill bear half right through a small gate onto a fenced path and follow this to a second gate and a cross path.

Shere is everything an English village should be and has many fine buildings. It is well worth taking the time to explore. Inn and church face each other across the village square where a young oak on the green has replaced the ancient elms that fell prey to Dutch Elm disease. A booklet describing the buildings and their history is for sale in the church. This too has several interesting features including a crusader chest, some venerable brasses and the top of a pilgrim's staff. In the 14th century the church had its own hermit or anchoress. In 1329 Christine, daughter of the local carpenter, was walled up in a cell attached to the church at her own request, 'to serve Almighty God more worthily'. Look for two openings in the north wall of the chancel. These were her only communication with the outside world. Through the roughly cross-shaped opening or quatrefoil she received communion and the slanted opening or squint enabled her to see the altar. After three years she left her cell. We do not know why and this breaking of a holy vow would have been considered a grave matter, usually leading to excommunication. Whatever the reason, she was allowed to be re-enclosed, to meditate on her 'nefarious sin'. We do not know how long she lived and whether she ended her days walled away from the world in what must have been unsanitary conditions. In those days disregard for such matters was seen as a demonstration of extreme piety.

8. Turn left.

9. At a cross track in front of a house called 'The Old Barn', turn left and follow the track round to a road. Cross the road and go ahead to a second road. Turn left, signed 'Dorking'.

10. Take the first lane on the right, Tower Hill, passing under the railway after a few yards. Some 25 yards after the arch turn left on a signed bridleway. Just after a farmhouse on the right, where a wooden fence on the left ends, bear left off the track on a clear path that leads to a track.

11. Turn left to the A25. Turn left under the railway, then take the first right back to the station car park. (If you started the walk in Shere, turn right along the A25 and continue from point 2.)

Gomshall is often shown as Gumshall on old maps. The atmosphere would not have been so pleasant in those days as the village was a centre of the tanning industry, notorious for being smelly. Gomshall Mill, now a restaurant, and the tannery made use of the Tilling Bourne that flows through the village and on through Shere to join the Wey at Shalford.

Walk 12
THE WEY NAVIGATION AND RIPLEY

This is a very easy and pleasant walk that explores the many water features of this level corner of the county. It starts and finishes along the Wey Navigation, where you can watch canal craft negotiate the locks. There is more waterside walking by a flooded sand pit. This sounds like a scar on the landscape but it has formed an attractive lake, rich in wildlife and alive with dinghies. The route then visits the historic and interesting village of Ripley for tea at a traditional bakery before the path returns to the canal for the final stretch, which passes the romantic ruins of a priory.

 Watson's has been a baker's shop for at least 125 years and the site had associations with baking in the 17th century: part of the present building dates from that period, Behind the shop is a delightful traditional tea room with the doors and frame of the old bread ovens. You can choose something from the tempting display in the shop to enjoy with your tea. For lunch there is a good selection of sandwiches and rolls or a ploughman's lunch, filled jacket potatoes and pasties. The all-day breakfast is satisfying and one suggestion is scrambled eggs with smoked salmon. They are open every day except Sunday and bank holidays until 5 pm throughout the year. Telephone: 01483 224332.

When the teashop is closed there are several attractive old inns in Ripley serving food.

DISTANCE: 4½ miles.

MAP: OS Explorer 145 Guildford and Farnham.

STARTING POINT: Car park on the south side of the Wey Navigation on the B367 (GR 039573).

HOW TO GET THERE: The B367 is the Ripley–West Byfleet road and the car park is about ½ mile south of Pyrford Village.

ALTERNATIVE STARTING POINT: If you wish to visit the teashop at the beginning or end of your walk, start in Ripley where there is ample parking in the car park by the village green. The teashop is on the other side of the other side of the main road, as you emerge from the green. You will then start the walk at point 7.

THE WALK

1. Walk to the far end of the car park and take a path that leads back to the road. Turn left for 25 yards then left again along the Wey Navigation towpath. At the first lock, Papercourt Lock, cross a bridge over the Navigation to continue along the towpath on the other side, passing in front of the lock cottage.

The Wey Navigation dates from an Act of Parliament in 1651 and opened in 1653. It was one of the first British rivers to be made navigable. Timber, coal, corn, flour, wood and even gunpowder from Chilworth (see Walk 10) were regularly moved up and down the waterway. The Wey, unlike many other less efficient waterways, survived the railway era and under private ownership continued to trade until well after the Second World War. The last owners, Stevens and Sons, donated the Wey to the National Trust in 1964.

2. At the next bridge, Tanyard Bridge, recross the canal and follow a surfaced path to shortly reach a lane. Turn left for 50 yards. Take an unsigned path on the right then turn left after five yards on a path parallel with the lane. In front of a stream turn right to walk with the stream on your left. Follow the path through a copse and past a pond on the right. Level with the end of the pond the path forks; bear right to a bridge on the left. Cross the bridge and turn right, now walking with the stream on your right.

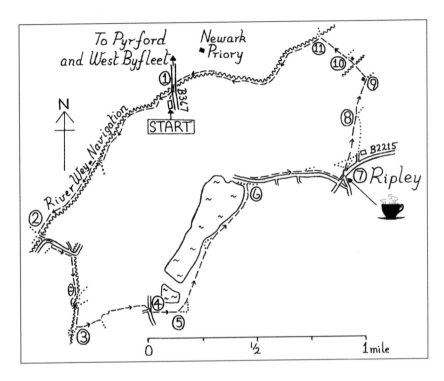

3. At the end of a field on the left, turn left along the edge of the field. (If you reach a bridge across the stream, you have gone 25 yards too far.) Continue round the edge of the field, passing a signed path over a footbridge on the right and some allotments on the left, to a lane.

4. Turn right for 40 yards then left on a signed path for 225 yards.

5. Bear left and follow the path through a belt of woodland to the bank of a lake. Press on with the lake on your left.

Papercourt Lake is a flooded sand pit, now the attractive home of a successful sailing club.

6. At the end of the lake bear right to a road. Turn right along the footway beside the road into Ripley. Turn left along the main road for a few yards to the teashop at the junction of High Street and Rose Lane.

7. From the teashop cross the High Street and take a short road opposite leading onto the village green. Continue across the green in the same direction, shortly crossing a track and passing to the left of a children's play area, to eventually reach a surfaced track.

Ripley originated as a small community round a crossroads. When Henry VIII developed Portsmouth as a naval port, the village was well placed to exploit the increased traffic on the highway and many of the pubs started life as coaching inns. By the mid 18th century the journey from London to Portsmouth by coach could be made in nine hours but many changes of horses were needed to accomplish this and the Talbot was one of the most important staging posts. Ripley has many fine Georgian buildings that date from this period of prosperity. This traffic ended with the coming of the railway and the village suffered lean times until the car returned traffic to the main Portsmouth road, the A3. The High Street was almost strangled by traffic until a bypass relieved the congestion in 1976. The bicycle was even more important than the car for Ripley's renaissance as the village became a favourite destination for cyclists who thronged its pubs and tea rooms.

8. Turn left.

9. Immediately after the last house on the left turn left again.

10. Opposite a pair of semi-detached cottages bear left off the track, shown by a yellow arrow on a post. Follow the path to regain the Navigation at a weir.

11. Do not cross the river but turn left along the towpath. Cross the river at the next lock and continue along the towpath to the road at a bridge. Turn left back to the start.

Newark Priory, across the river on private land, was founded in 1189 by Ruald de Clane and his wife Beatrice of Send and dedicated to the Virgin Mary and Thomas à Becket. When King Henry VIII dissolved the monastery in 1539 the Prior was pensioned off and valuables sent to the Tower of London. It is said that a cannon was employed to demolish the extensive buildings.

Walk 13
ESHER COMMONS

This delightful walk wends its way across the commons south of Esher to a National Trust garden and tea room. The walk is not long so a good plan for an all-day expedition is to do the first leg in the morning, lunch at the teashop then explore Claremont Landscape Garden before strolling back to the start. Almost all the route is within woods but the composition of the woodland changes as the walk progresses, reflecting the history of different areas. Surprisingly, there are one or two good viewpoints across the Mole valley. The route is mostly easy going and fairly level but there are two very short but very sharp little climbs, one near the start and one soon after Claremont: just enough to justify a good tea.

 A good tea is what you can be sure of at a National Trust tea room. The speciality of the house at Claremont Landscape Garden is apple or pear charlotte served with cream or ice cream. This is in honour of Princess Charlotte, daughter of George IV, who lived at Claremont following her marriage in 1816. There is a tempting selection of cakes and biscuits for tea and cream teas include clotted cream. Lunch is served between noon and 2 pm and you can choose between sandwiches and filled jacket potatoes or daily specials listed on the board. There are some tables outside on a sheltered, hedged patio. The tea room is open every day except Monday (open bank holidays) from 11 am until 5 pm from the beginning of April until the end of October. In November and for the first half of December it closes on Tuesday as well. It closes entirely for the second half of December and first half of January and then re-opens at weekends until the end of March. Telephone: 01372 469421.

DISTANCE: 4½ miles.
MAP: OS Explorer 161 London South.
STARTING POINT: Copsem Lane car park (GR 140626).
HOW TO GET THERE: Copsem Lane car park is on the A244 between Esher and Leatherhead, about 200 yards north of its junction with the A3.
ALTERNATIVE STARTING POINT: If you wish to visit the teashop at the beginning or end of your walk, start at West End Lane car park. You will then start the walk at point 9.

THE WALK

1. There are many paths at the rear of the car park and the secret of this walk is to start along the correct one. Go to the notice board. Facing it, go left for 15 yards and the path at this point is the one you want; there is a wooden post in the middle of the path after a couple of yards, and after 15 yards it goes across a ditch and up two shallow earth steps. Some 40 yards further on the path forks; bear left. After 100 yards the path rises up some more steps. Ignore a path on the left and continue uphill up further steps. At the top follow the path ahead, along the top of a wooded ridge. Go over a broad track and press on to a T-junction.

If you had walked here two hundred years ago the landscape would have looked very different. Most of this area was open heathland, used for grazing. During the 19th century changes in farming led to a decline in grazing. This allowed woodland to spread and, in addition, Scots pine was planted for timber. Despite some felling during both World Wars and a large fire during the 1920s, the woodland has spread so that today the commons are mainly wooded. The commons are managed to enhance their value for wildlife and for public recreation.

2. Turn right. The path shortly bears left so you are still walking in

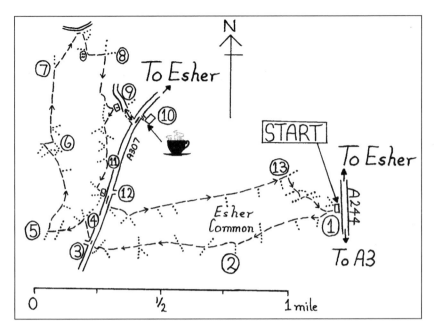

the same direction. Cross three tracks to eventually join a track coming in from the left. Turn right for a few yards, towards a main road. Just before the road bear right to emerge on the road opposite the entrance to 'The Homewood'.

This road was an important route into London for merchants. 'Coal and Wine' tax posts were set up on all roads where they crossed into the Metropolitan Police District in the 19th century and importers had to pay dues to the City Corporation to be used for the support of the orphan children of London citizens. The tax was discontinued in the 1890s.

3. Turn right for a few yards to pick up a path on the left, signed 'Winterdown Road 1M', and follow this for 200 yards.

4. Just before some pylons turn sharp left on a cross path. Follow this over a cross path and on for a further 50 yards to a T-junction.

5. Turn right and follow the path along the edge of a cliff to a fence at the edge of the wood. Having diverted left to the viewpoint with a seat conveniently placed to admire the view, follow the main path round to the right to a T-junction.

Margy Pond

The cliff has been eroded by a meander in the river Mole and it is obvious in places that this process is still continuing. This is a notable area of ancient woodland. This does not mean that it has survived untouched but that there has been continuous woodland cover for many centuries, unlike most of the commons.

6. Turn left to walk with woods on the right and a field on the left.

7. Some 20 yards after the track becomes surfaced turn right on a track. Just before a lane bear right for 20 yards parallel with the lane then turn right and follow the main path to Margy Pond. Bear round to the left of the pond and carry on along the main path to a clear cross path.

8. Turn right. As the path emerges from the wood bear left at a fork, immediately after a seat on the left. This leads to West End Lane car park and a lane.

☕ **9.** Turn right to a road junction. The entrance to Claremont Park is a few yards to the left and the tea room is on the right along the entrance drive.

During the 18th century some of the most eminent architects and gardeners shaped Claremont into one of England's outstanding gardens. Sir John Vanbrugh started by building a house here. He sold it to the Duke of Newcastle and William Kent extended the garden. The estate was sold to Clive of India in 1768 and Capability Brown, who also worked on the garden, built a new house. Clive was fabulously rich: Horace Walpole wrote, 'General Clive has arrived, all over estates and diamonds'. He is reputed to have spent £100,000, a vast sum in those days, though he never lived here. In 1816 it became the home of Prince Leopold and his bride, Princess Charlotte, daughter of George IV. Sadly, the princess, a girl of 21, died with her baby the following year. The future Queen Victoria was a frequent visitor to her Uncle Leopold and spent her birthdays at Claremont for the first ten years of her reign. The house is now a girls' school. Claremont condenses into only 50 acres most of the features beloved of the 18th century – lake, island, temple, belvedere and grotto – as well as an unusual turf amphitheatre. The clipped and mown perfection of Claremont today is the result of a massive restoration undertaken by the National Trust in the 1970s. This involved clearing laurels and rhododendrons up to 30 feet high that had rampaged over much of the garden. It is open almost every day, closing on Mondays in the winter. Telephone: 01372 467806.

10. Return to West End Lane car park and now take a gravel track at the rear of the car park. As you approach trees take a path on the left 10 yards after a path on the right. Follow this over a cross path then very steeply uphill. At the top of the slope follow the path along the top of the slope on the right.

11. When the path forks bear left to a T-junction. Turn left to Horseshoe Clump car park and the main road.

12. Turn right for 60 yards to a path and bridleway on the left. Turn left along the footpath, signed 'Oxshott Heath 1¼M', to a cross path. Turn left. Continue ahead at the first track on the right, signed 'Arbrook Common ¾M', and the second, signed 'Arbrook Common ½M', to a third, waymarked by blue arrows on a post but with no signpost.

13. Turn right and follow the path under the power lines to a T-junction. Turn left for 70 yards then turn right and follow this path back to the car park where the walk started.

Walk 14
NORBURY PARK

This very pleasant walk is almost entirely within the boundaries of Norbury Park, an estate of woods and farms bought by Surrey County Council in 1930 to protect it from development. The going is easy on well-maintained paths and tracks. The outward leg is mainly through woods and partly follows a woodland trail that illustrates aspects of woodland management. The return is more open and there is the bonus of a splendid view near the end.

The Old Barn Tea Room at Bocketts Farm near Leatherhead is housed in a large 18th century farm building with extensive seating outside as well. There is a good selection of cakes on offer. They are all encased in plastic boxes in the interests of hygiene as so many visitors may have been handling animals but are none the less delicious, and on my visit I was intrigued by a subtle and interesting elderflower sponge. Possibilities for lunch range from sandwiches and filled jacket potatoes to full meals such as quiche or pasta bake and a full English breakfast is served all day. They are open all year from 10 am until 6 pm, closing earlier in winter. Telephone: 01372 363764.

DISTANCE: 4½ miles.
MAP: OS Explorer 146 Dorking, Box Hill and Reigate.
STARTING POINT: Crabtree Lane car park near Westhumble (GR 158524).
HOW TO GET THERE: Follow the A24 and 2½ miles south of its junction with the A246 take a minor road west, signed 'Westhumble Station'. Immediately after the station bear right on a little lane for ½ mile to a car park on the right.
ALTERNATIVE STARTING POINT: If you wish to visit the teashop at the beginning or end of your walk, start at Bocketts Farm Park on the A246 south of Leatherhead. The teashop is to the left at the entrance and there is ample parking. You will then start the walk at point 6.

THE WALK

1. Take a path from the rear of the car park and follow it gently uphill and then down to join a surfaced track coming in from the right. Continue in the same direction. A diversion from the track to a signed viewpoint over the Mole valley to Box Hill is well worth taking and a path returns you to the track a little farther on.

The woodland of Norbury Park is actively managed to enhance the landscape, provide for wildlife and to produce timber. The sawmill passed on the left produces notice boards, benches, gates and so on for Surrey County Council.

Norbury Park mansion may be glimpsed to the right. It is in private ownership. Designed in very grand style in the late 18th century, a magnificent painted room was created soon after it was built. As if the local views were not good enough, this depicted scenes from the Lake District, as seen through a window. A previous owner was Dr Marie Stopes, the sex education pioneer, who lived here with her husband, the aircraft designer Sir Alliott Verdon Roe.

2. When the surfaced track bends right at a small picnic area on the left, continue ahead, bearing right at a fork after 15 yards, signed 'To the sculpture'. Press on ahead when a similar track joins from the right 50 yards after the sculpture.

Despite the depredations of previous owners and the devastating effects of the storm of 1987, some 500 acres of Norbury Park are woodland. Posts with letters on the left of the track refer to a nature trail illustrating aspects

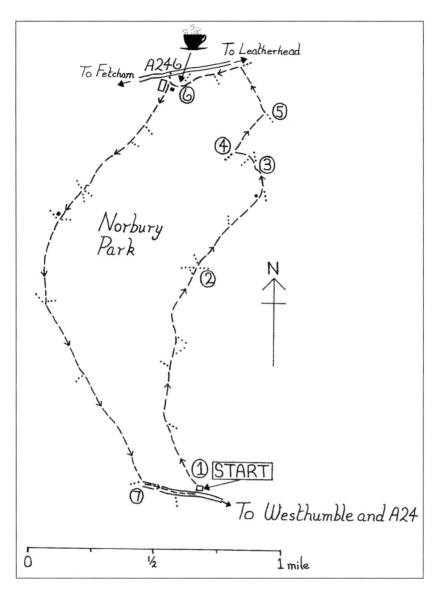

To Leatherhead

To Fetcham A246

To Westhumble and A24

START

Norbury Park

N

0 ½ 1 mile

of woodland ecology. H draws your attention to a new plantation of beech. They were planted in the early 1980s along with larch and spruce, which sheltered the beech until they were established. These 'nurse' trees have now been removed. G refers to the complex structure of woodland, which has four layers of vegetation, each with its associated animal life.

Trefoil sculpture

The top layer is the canopy (oak and sweet chestnut here). Next comes the shrub layer of hazel and birch scrub. Lower still is the field layer of brambles and at the bottom is the ground layer of grasses, moss and fungi. Point F is where there is natural regeneration of trees, in this case birch, following the loss in 1987. Despite this natural recovery, the area is being managed by thinning the trees to maintain diversity.

The sculpture on the left is called Trefoil. Steve Geliot created it from a giant cedar that fell in the great storm referred to above. It exemplifies the contrast between the size of the trees, the minute details of their structure and the changing nature of the spaces between them.

3. Bear left at a fork and follow the main track, ignoring a track on the left, to just before the track bends sharp left at a seat overlooking farmland.

The manor of Norbury is referred to in the Domesday Book. It had many owners down the centuries until 1766, when it was bought by Anthony Chapman. He cut down much of the woodland, especially the magnificent walnuts for which it was famous. They were sold to make gunstocks for the British Army. It was again on the market in 1930. In those days planning powers were much weaker than today and the advertising suggested it would make a suitable site for development. To prevent this a local councillor, Alderman Willcocks, bought it and then sold it on to Surrey County Council. To confirm the purchase and allow it to intervene when similar threats arose again, the Council obtained the Surrey County Council Act in 1931, which gave it greater control of development. The estate of 1,340 acres today consists of three small tenanted farms – Norbury Park (dairy), Swansworth (sheep) and Bocketts Farm, run as a farm park.

4. Turn right on a signed path and follow it steeply downhill to a small gate into a field.

☕ **5.** Through the gate turn left to walk along the left hand side of the field. At the end of the field turn left over a stile beside a field gate and follow the path ahead to Bocketts Farm and the teashop.

6. Turn right out of the teashop then turn left just before the car park. Follow this track for almost 2 miles, ignoring all side turns, to reach a T-junction.

This track passes two more points of the woodland trail. Point M refers to the need to fence stock to maintain woods. Much of England was originally covered by woodland. Some was deliberately cut down to clear land for farming or for the timber but most was lost because it was grazed. The sheep and cows nibble the young tree seedlings so the wood cannot regenerate and it disappears.

At point L there is an example of the traditional method of woodland management, known as coppice with standards. Hazel was cut back to provide wood for fuel and small uses and then allowed to sprout again for 20 years or so, forming the coppice. In between large trees or standards were allowed to grow to maturity to provide major timber. This coppice is now ready for harvesting and it is hoped to reintroduce this kind of management.

7. Turn left, signed 'Westhumble', and follow the lane back to the start.

Walk 15
RANMORE COMMON

Ranmore Common is deservedly popular as a walking area and this route has everything for which you could wish. It starts with a mile or so through woodland, attractive at any time of year and doubly so in spring when the woods are carpeted with flowers. Having passed the famous Youth Hostel at Tanners Hatch it wends its way along the valley floor and over the hillside to the largest vineyard in England, where there is a striking, modern visitor centre and tea room. The main feature of the return leg is the ever-improving views, saving the best till last.

The restaurant at Denbies Vineyard north of Dorking, in a magnificent atrium in the centre of the building and roofed in glass, is very attractive and most unusual. The tiled floor and plants give the feeling of outdoors and yet it is comfortable in all weathers, with big fans and sunshades in summer. They offer delicious cakes and pastries as well as an enterprising selection of sandwiches in a range of breads, soup and their own interpretation of a ploughman's – a Vineyard Worker's lunch.

Hot meals are served between noon and 2 pm. Perhaps not quite the thing to suggest in a book of teashop walks, but you can always try the local produce as a change from tea. They are open throughout the year until 5.30 pm. Telephone: 01306 876616.

During the summer months of June, July and August tea and cakes are served on Sunday between 2 pm and 4 pm in the churchyard at Ranmore Common to raise funds to help maintain the fabric of the building.

DISTANCE: 5½ miles.
MAP: OS Explorer 146 Dorking, Box Hill and Reigate.
STARTING POINT: Denbies Hillside car park, Ranmore Common Road (National Trust, charge) (GR 142503).
HOW TO GET THERE: From the A24 on the northern edge of Dorking at Ashcombe School take a minor road, signed 'Guildford (A25) Business Park'. At a mini-roundabout continue ahead, signed 'Ranmore Effingham', to a T-junction. Turn right for about a mile to the National Trust car park on the left.
ALTERNATIVE STARTING POINT: If you wish to visit the teashop at the beginning or end of your walk, start at Denbies Vineyard where there is a large car park. Permission should be sought before leaving a car for a long period. The teashop is in the visitor centre. You will then start the walk at point 11.

The Walk

1. Cross the road and turn left on a path between the wood and the road for about 200 yards, crossing two tracks.

2. At the third track, by Fox Cottages, turn right, signed 'Youth Hostel'. Follow the track downhill and turn right past Tanners Hatch Youth Hostel.

During the Second World War a couple of hostellers were cycling on Ranmore Common. They spotted an apple tree laden with fruit, and broke through the undergrowth to claim the harvest. They found a couple of abandoned cottages. Eventually permission was granted to make these into a youth hostel and this was done between 1944 and 1946. Fittings such as sinks and windows were reclaimed from bomb-damaged buildings. Whenever an odd shaped piece of timber was needed, the restorers bent a length of wire to the shape needed and wandered round the woods until a match was found, and apparently these structural renovations are still in place today.

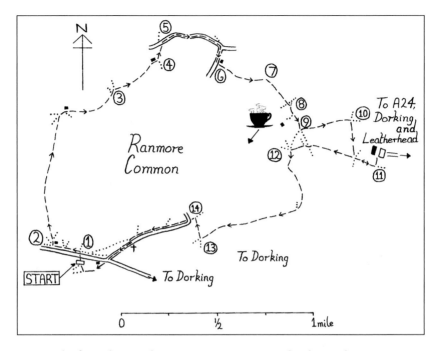

3. Just before the track starts to rise, turn right through a gate onto a grassy path, waymarked by a blue arrow on a post. Follow the path across a field to farm buildings then on, through a small gate, to a T-junction.

4. Turn left.

5. At a lane turn right. Take the first lane on the right, signed 'Ranmore Common', for 180 yards.

6. Just after the last cottage on the left, turn left on a signed path and walk along the left hand side of a field. As you approach the end of the field, do not go through a gate on the left but press on for a further 15 yards to the corner to find, at the time of writing, a rather broken down stile giving onto a narrow path along the edge of a wood. This leads up to a stile into a field.

7. Over the stile head half right across the field to find a stile about 20 yards uphill from a metal field gate. Over this stile cross a path immediately and go ahead for 25 yards to a T-junction with a track.

74

8. Turn right. When the track bends sharp right to Ashleigh Grange continue ahead on a rougher track to a T-junction.

9. Turn left.

10. At a cross path turn right, signed 'Dorking 1¼'. Shortly go through a gate into the vineyard and ahead between vines to a track. Turn left and immediately fork right along a surfaced drive to the winery and teashop on the left.

Denbies Wine Estate is the largest vineyard in England with over 200 acres planted with vines and it alone is 10% of the English area under viniculture. This creates unusual views with some vistas being more reminiscent of France than Surrey. The first vines were planted in 1986 and they grow several types and produce a variety of wines, which have won an impressive array of awards. There are examples of all the types of vine planted in the cloister behind the restaurant. Tours of the winery are available (charge), ending in a tasting.

11. Return along the drive to the point where you joined it. Now continue ahead along a concrete track and follow it up as far as a sharp right hand bend. On the bend bear left on an unsurfaced track and climb up to a cross track.

12. Turn left. This is the North Downs Way. Follow it for nearly a mile to a cross track. As you walk up this track, views to the left across the Mole valley to Box Hill gradually open up.

13. Turn right, still signed 'North Downs Way'.

14. At a T-junction with a concrete drive turn left to join a lane at a corner and press on along the lane in the same direction, using a path between the lane and a wood on the right. At Ranmore church rejoin the lane and carry on to a T-junction. Though in sight of the car park, for a final magnificent view cross the road to carry on along the North Downs Way on a path to the left of a house. Go through a gate and turn right then bear right to a gate into the rear of the car park.

Walk 16
LEITH HILL

This superb circuit includes all that makes walking in this part of Southern England such a pleasure. Most of the route lies within woodland and also visits an ancient village with a good pub and a tucked-away hamlet with pretty cottages. Pine trees thrive on the light, sandy soil and the scent on a warm summer's day is positively heady. The objective is Leith Hill, the highest point in south-east England, and, of course, this cannot be attained without some climbing. But it is not too taxing, coming in three bursts separated by long level sections. Once you reach the top of the hill the views are spectacular, even more so from the top of the tower, open to the public. This walk is enjoyable in all seasons but, above all, choose a clear day and you might see the sea and St Paul's.

Leith Hill Tower is in the care of the National Trust and the refreshment, though limited in scope, is of excellent quality. There is a selection of delicious cakes and shortbread supplemented by sandwiches. There is no indoor accommodation or chairs and tables – take your tea to your chosen spot on the picnic site and enjoy the fabulous views as you eat. The tower is open on Wednesdays, weekends and Bank Holiday Mondays between the end of March and the end of September from 10 am until 5 pm and fine weekends in winter, closing at 3.30 pm. Telephone: 01306 711777.

When the servery at the tower is closed the pub in Coldharbour, the Plough, is directly on the route and serves good food.

DISTANCE: 5 miles.
MAP: OS Explorer 146 Dorking, Box Hill and Reigate.
STARTING POINT: Broadmoor Hill car park (GR 132454).
HOW TO GET THERE: From the A25 between Guildford and Dorking, just over a mile east of Abinger Hammer take a minor road south, Hollow Lane signed 'Abinger Common Friday Street Leith Hill', for 1¼ miles. Take the first lane left, signed 'Friday Street'. Go ahead at the first junction and right at the second, signed 'Leith Hill', to a car park on the left after 250 yards.
ALTERNATIVE STARTING POINT: There is no road access to the tower and hence no alternative start.

THE WALK

1. Return to the lane and turn right. Walk back to the junction and bear right for 80 yards to a cross path.

2. Turn right. Bear right after 120 yards and follow the path down through the woods to a T-junction. Turn right for 85 yards then left to a lane in the hamlet of Broadmoor.

3. Turn left for 120 yards. Opposite the entrance to the Triple Bar Riding Centre turn right along a track signed as a public bridleway. Bear left off the track after 70 yards and the path cuts through to another track. Turn left. At the entrance to Tillingbourne Cottage continue ahead, uphill and initially between wire fences to meet a sandy cross track.

4. Turn right. When the track forks, bear right, protected by a low barrier, and this eventually rejoins the main track. Continue in the same direction and soon bear right again onto a parallel path. This too eventually rejoins the main track. Press on in the same direction to a lane in Coldharbour.

This track is a BOAT – a byway open to all traffic or a road that never got

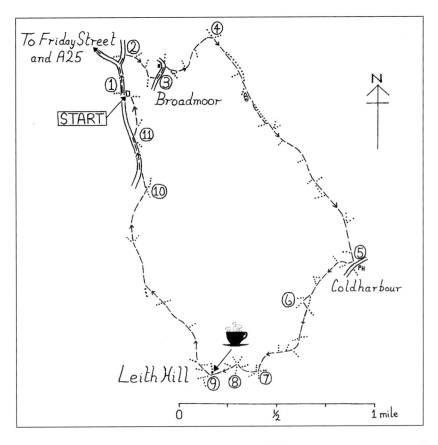

surfaced. As such, it is open to motorised vehicles as well as horses and walkers so you might meet the occasional off-road vehicle or motorcycle. They can churn the track up and hence the parallel walkers' paths.

5. Turn right, uphill, along a track. Bear right at a fork after 80 yards. The first view soon opens up on the left, with a seat well placed to admire it. Carry on up to the cricket pitch, where the track forks.

Coldharbour is the highest village in Surrey, 750 feet up on the side of Leith Hill. The cricket pitch must have the most spectacular views of any in the country, sweeping south across the Weald. Can the players concentrate on their match? Does it give the home team an advantage?

6. Just before an information board turn left on a footpath waymarked with a green arrow. Turn right at a cross path, following the green waymarks. When the waymarked trail bears right, continue ahead on the larger path, soon picking up the green arrows again.

7. At a cross path turn right, still with the green waymarks and passing between three short wooden posts. After 15 yards a track joins on the right and the way ahead immediately forks; bear right.

☕ **8.** At a complex junction of tracks and paths turn left **uphill** to Leith Tower and its tea kiosk.

Leith Hill is the crown of Surrey at 965 feet and a matchless place to stand and see the world at your feet. There is nothing as high between the hill and the sea to the south or east and the nearest rival height to the west is in the Mendips, 100 miles away. It rises above the North Downs and beyond those hills the ridge of the Chilterns can be picked out, 50 miles away. To the south is the patchwork plain of the Weald and then the South Downs with perhaps a glimpse of the sea through Shoreham Gap. It is recorded that in 1844, on a clear day, a group of Ordnance Surveyors looking out from here with their 'small glass' saw 41 of London's church towers and were able to pick out a staff four inches thick on Dunstable Downs, 50 miles away. Richard Hull of Leith Hill Place loved this spot and built the tower in 1766, apparently to take it over 1,000 feet above sea level. It is now in the care of the National Trust, who restored it from a dilapidated state. You can climb to the top at 1,029 feet (charge) and the views are even more spectacular. Richard Hull was buried beneath his creation.

9. Go to the far side of the tower and turn right at the end of the picnic area. When the path forks after 125 yards, bear right, ignoring a small path on the right. Bear right again at a second fork after a further 110 yards. Ignore all side turns to eventually merge with a major path coming in from the left and continue in the same direction. At a three-way fork take the middle path to continue gently downhill to reach a track on a sharp bend.

10. Turn left, slightly uphill, to a lane. Turn right.

11. Watch for two paths on the right. Take the second one, opposite a signed path on the left. Bear round to the left to walk more or less parallel with the lane on an increasingly obvious path and this leads back to the car park.

Walk 17
EPSOM DOWNS AND WALTON ON THE HILL

This interesting walk starts at the famous Tattenham Corner of Epsom Downs racecourse and crosses the downs to the pretty village of Walton on the Hill where a teashop overlooks the village pond. I suggest you plan to walk this route in the morning, visiting the teashop for lunch. There are two reasons for this recommendation. Firstly, racehorses train on the gallops before noon so you may have the thrilling sight of them in full flight. Secondly, the teashop offers an exceptional range of tasty sandwiches. Do not even think of doing this walk on race days, especially during the Derby meeting in June.

 The Picnic Basket at Walton on the Hill is a lively and friendly establishment offering a wonderful range of sandwich fillings that may be enjoyed on white or brown bread, in a baguette, on grilled pannini or in a tortilla wrap. The same fillings can be taken with a jacket potato and there is also a daily special. To finish with there is a small selection of cakes and Danish pastries. They also sell a tempting choice of jams and pickles in the delicatessen section. The Picnic Basket is open every day throughout the year from 8.30 am during the week, 9.30 am on Saturday and 10.30 am on Sunday. They close at 5 pm except during the darkest days of winter, when they close a little earlier. Telephone: 01737 814171.

DISTANCE: 5 miles.
MAP: OS Explorer 146 Dorking, Box Hill and Reigate.
STARTING POINT: Tattenham Corner car park (GR 224584).
HOW TO GET THERE: The car park is on the B290, the Epsom-Tadworth road.
ALTERNATIVE STARTING POINT: If you wish to visit the teashop at the beginning or end of your walk, start in Walton on the Hill where there is some street parking. The teashop is in the centre of the village, almost opposite the pond. You will then start the walk at point 6.

THE WALK
1. Cross the B290 and take a surfaced drive opposite the car park. When this bends left continue in the same direction across the racecourse on an obvious path. Recross the racecourse and carry on ahead, now on a track.

In the early 17th century Epsom was famous as a spa town, drawing fashionable society including Charles II and his court and Samuel Pepys. It had been observed that cattle would not drink from a local spring and tests showed the water was rich in magnesium sulphate, now commonly called Epsom Salts. This was believed to be good for the health, especially indigestion, but, if we believe Pepys, taking the waters was just an excuse for a party. There was 'a public breakfast, dancing and music every morning at the Wells'. Pepys also records in his diary for 25 May 1663 'a great throng going to the Downs upon a great horse and foot race'. As taking the water fell out of fashion in the 18th century racing became more important and regular meetings were established by 1730. The grandstand was built in 1927 and has a minor place in architectural history as the first structure of its kind to be built of reinforced concrete.

2. When the track bends sharp right, go ahead on a signed bridleway, which soon bears right itself. Ignore paths left and right to shortly come to a cross path. Turn right and immediately left to carry on in the same direction on a surfaced track to a complex junction with one path ahead, one right and three to the left.

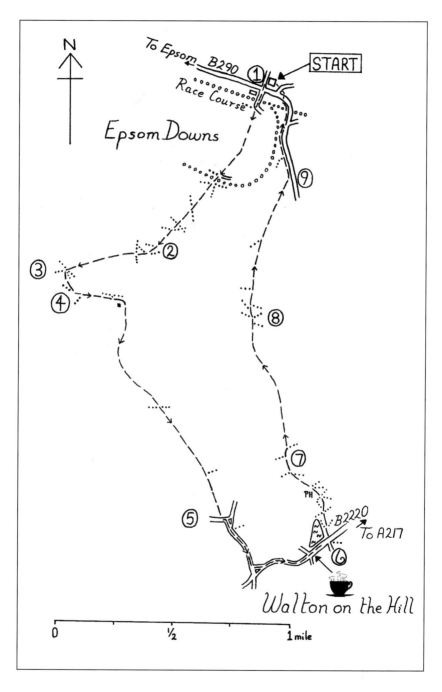

N

To Epsom B290

START

①

Race Course

Epsom Downs

⑨

②

③

④

⑧

⑦

PH

⑤

B2220
To A217

⑥

Walton on the Hill

0   ½   1 mile

3. Take the third path on the left – the one furthest from you. This leads through woods to a track in the bottom of the valley.

4. Turn left. Ignore a bridleway signed 'Walton Road ¾M' on the right after 25 yards. Press on ahead, signed 'Walton on the Hill 1½M', at a junction with a track on the left, soon passing an entrance to a farmhouse. Follow the signed bridleway round to the right. After about a mile it becomes a surfaced drive that shortly leads to a road.

5. Turn left. Ignore Ebbisham Lane immediately on the left and follow the road ahead into Walton on the Hill. Turn left at the main road to the teashop on the right.

6. Turn right out of the teashop. At the end of the pond turn left. When the track forks after 30 yards take the right branch, not the bridleway also forking right at this point. Continue past the Bell to a metal barrier. Go past this and press on in the same direction, now downhill with a wooden fence on the left, to join a track on a bend.

7. Turn right. Take a public bridleway on the left, signed 'Epsom Lane North 1¼M'.

8. Just after a series of metal posts on the right, the path forks: bear left. When it forks again after a further 40 yards, bear right. There is another junction after a further 50 yards; this time keep ahead, signed 'Epsom Lane North ½M'. The path eventually joins a track. Turn right to continue in the same direction and eventually reach a road.

9. Turn left back to the start.

In 1779 a group of aristocratic racing enthusiasts, led by Lord Derby, established a race for three year old fillies. They called the race The Oaks, after the Derbys' family home. This was followed a year later by the famous Derby, a race for three year old colts, that first took place on 4 May 1780. It was named after the race's co-founder on the toss of a coin. Had the coin fallen the other way the classic race would be the Bunbury!

Walk 18
TILBURSTOW HILL AND GODSTONE

This route is a gentle amble round part of the greensand ridge. It is varied and interesting and calls in at the ancient community of Godstone for refreshment overlooking the village green with its large duckpond. There are many attractive views and one outstanding panorama right at the start. The walk passes several ponds and the last few hundred yards cross a nature reserve on the site of a sandstone quarry. It is very interesting to see how nature repairs the scars man makes upon the earth so you cannot see the damage once done, clothed as it is in lovely woodland, carpeted with flowers in spring.

 The Old Forge overlooks Godstone's delightful green and has some tables outside from which to watch the world go by in this busy village. A variety of snacks and light meals are served, including toasted sandwiches and filled jacket potatoes as well as a substantial breakfast, rounded off with a choice of cakes. They are open every day except Sunday throughout the year between 8 am and 4 pm during the week and 9 am and 5 pm on Saturday. Telephone: 01883 743230.

When the teashop is closed there are several pubs in Godstone that serve food.

DISTANCE: 4 miles.

MAP: OS Explorer 146 Dorking, Box Hill and Reigate.

STARTING POINT: Tilburstow Hill car park (GR 349501).

HOW TO GET THERE: From junction 6 of the M25 take the B2235 and drive through Godstone. Fork right, signed 'Tilburstow Hill'. Take the first lane on the right. There is a car park on the left after about ¼ mile.

ALTERNATIVE STARTING POINT: If you wish to visit the teashop at the beginning or end of your walk, start in Godstone where there is a car park on the village green. You are only allowed to park for three hours so don't dawdle too much! The teashop overlooks the green. You will then start the walk at point 7.

THE WALK

1. Leave the car park by a signed path at the rear that leads steeply down through woodland to a T-junction with a cross path.

2. Turn left. Cross a road slightly right to continue in the same direction. Ignore two signed paths on the right and continue to a cross path waymarked by yellow arrows on a post.

3. Turn right. After about 350 yards take a path on the right, again signed by yellow arrows, and follow it to a road.

4. Turn left for about 200 yards then right along a tiny lane, signed 'Footpath & Bridleway to Tandridge'. After 160 yards take a signed path on the left over a stile and follow a fenced path, ignoring a path on the right, to another stile and a T-junction with a track.

5. Turn left. When the track bends left turn right on a path along the left hand side of a field for 150 yards. Now turn left on a waymarked path that eventually leads through a churchyard to a lane.

St Nicholas' church is now about ½ mile from the centre of Godstone. Until the time of Elizabeth I this was the centre of the village but a Roman road, abandoned for centuries, was brought back into use and the village moved to exploit this new commercial opportunity. The medieval church survived this desertion and was heavily restored in the 19th century by Sir

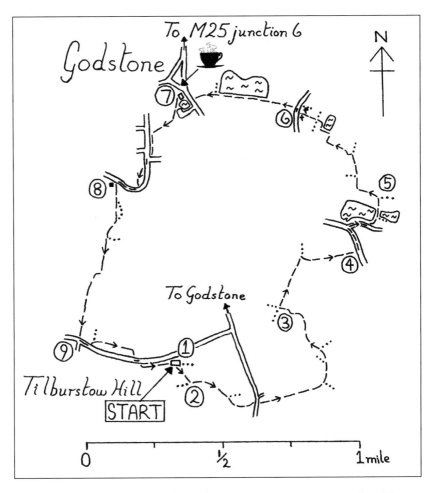

Giles Gilbert Scott, who lived locally. Many commentators judge this was not a resounding success. It is worth going a few yards left to look at a better-received project, St Mary's Homes and chapel. A local widow founded the almshouses in 1872 when her only daughter died young. A portrait of the unfortunate girl hangs in the chapel. There are eight attractive little cottages and a chapel clustered round three sides of a courtyard with a well. They are still lived in by elderly local people.

☕ **6.** Cross the lane right to continue in the same direction, now on a surfaced path leading past Bay Pond to emerge in Godstone opposite the village green and pond. Turn right to the teashop.

The village dates back to the Iron Age though its centre has shifted, as explained above. The focal point of the modern settlement is the attractive village green, complete with pond and cricket pitch. In the 16th century it was a centre of gunpowder production and Bay Pond was originally created to provide the head of water to power a mill. It is now a nature reserve. Godstone has a splendid collection of ancient pubs including the White Hart, which was once a famous coaching inn and is said to date back to the time of Richard II. His insignia was a white hart. It is supposed to have been visited by several crowned heads, including the Czar of Russia in 1815 when he was on his way to a boxing match at nearby Blindley Heath.

7. From the teashop take a path to the right of the pond then bear right on a path beside the green. At the end of the green turn left and walk out of the village; use a signed footpath on the right to avoid walking along the road. When this rejoins the road, continue in the same direction.

8. At a house called 'Eden Brook' turn left along the drive to Garston Park. Follow the drive up until it bends left. Go over a stile on the right to continue in the same direction on a fenced path to a second stile. Over the stile turn right then bear left to follow a clear path uphill to a lane.

9. Turn left along the lane for 100 yards then go through a gate on the left. When the path forks after few yards bear right. Follow the path through the woodland parallel with the lane to a similar gate on the right. Go through this back onto the lane and turn left for 35 yards to an unsigned path on the right. This leads back to the car park where this walk started.

This lovely woodland is on the site of an abandoned sandstone quarry, and is managed as a nature reserve. Many species of woodland flower are to be found in season. The most bizarre is the bird's nest orchid. It lives on rotting vegetation, which it exploits with the help of a fungus living in the soil, and is usually found in the densest and shadiest part of woodland, where other plants cannot survive. The name comes from its mass of roots, which are supposed to resemble a bird's nest.

Walk 19
WOLDINGHAM DOWNS

Wooded hillsides overlooking parkland, spectacular views and cool green paths full of bluebells in season combine to make this walk a superb example of the many routes that criss-cross the North Downs. About half the walk is in woodland protected by the Woodland Trust and there are some magnificent trees. Leaving the woodland the route drops to a secluded valley with a mansion and gardens associated with the anti-slavery campaigner William Wilberforce, now a school. The last part of the circuit returns to the woods and brings home what the term deciduous rain forest really means.

 The Dene Tea Room in Woldingham Road, to the west of Woldingham Garden Village, is to be found in the old house with tables indoors, in a conservatory or on a patio overlooking lovely gardens to a view beyond. It is connected to a garden centre by a most attractive pergola. There is a good selection of cakes and other teatime goodies including toasted teacakes and cream teas with clotted cream. For lunch there is a tempting range of sandwiches or filled jacket potatoes and salads supplemented by daily specials, both savoury and sweet. They are open throughout the year between 9.30 am and 4.30 pm during the week and 10 am and 4 pm at the weekend. Telephone: 01883 652712.

DISTANCE: 5 miles.
MAP: OS Explorer 146 Dorking, Box Hill and Reigate.
STARTING POINT: Marden Park Woods car park at South Hawke (GR 373541).
HOW TO GET THERE: Take the A25 and ½ mile east of its junction with the A22, near junction 6 of the M25, follow a minor lane, Tandridge Hill Lane, north to a T-junction. Turn right for about ¼ mile to a car park on the left.
ALTERNATIVE STARTING POINT: If you wish to visit the teashop at the beginning or end of your walk, start at Knights Garden Centre, Woldingham where there is ample parking but permission should be sought before leaving a car while you are walking. The teashop is signed. You will then start the walk at point 6.

THE WALK

1. Facing the lane take a path starting through a gap on the right hand side. When the path forks after 60 yards bear left. Follow the path up some steps to meet a track.

These woods are owned and managed by the Woodland Trust, a charity dedicated to conserving our native woodlands, just as much part of our heritage as great cathedrals and stately homes. Ancient woodland is home to hundreds of different types of animals, plants and fungi as well as the more obvious magnificent trees. The threat from the demands of development, overuse and dumping of rubbish is constant. Like the better-known National Trust, the Woodland Trust extends protection by owning the sites and providing skilled management.

2. Turn left and walk along the track to a T-junction.

3. Turn right. After about 150 yards follow the main track as it turns sharp left and heads gently downhill. Stay on the main path, following yellow waymarks, to a stile out of the wood. Now follow a grassy path round to the right and downhill to a stile onto a drive.

The building in the valley below is Woldingham School, a Catholic boarding school for girls. It is now in lay management but was previously

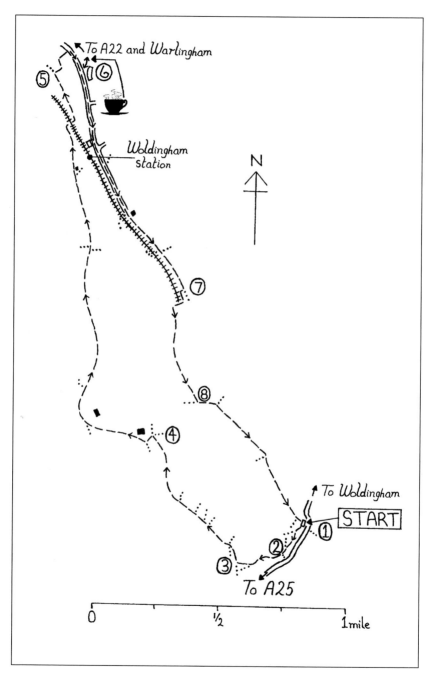

the Convent of the Sacred Heart. The red brick pile was constructed in 1880 on the site of a 17th century mansion built by Sir Robert Clayton (1629–1707), a wealthy merchant and Lord Mayor of London. It was later the home of William Wilberforce (1759–1833), the MP who devoted himself to the abolition of slavery.

4. Turn left. At a T-junction turn right and walk past school buildings and continue along the drive. When it forks at a white house, bear left. Go under a railway bridge and carry on for about 400 yards.

☕ **5.** Turn right on a signed path to a road. Turn right to the teashop, just before Knights Garden Centre, on the left.

6. Return to the road, turn left and walk as far as Woldingham Station. Continue in the same direction on a lane, Church Road, pressing on when it becomes a track after farm buildings on the left.

7. At a sign saying you are ¾ mile from Woldingham Station turn right over a stile, signed 'Woldingham Countryside Walk', and follow the clear path through dense woods to a T-junction.

If you had flown across England three thousand years ago you would have seen a dense forest across almost the whole land – temperate deciduous forest. Over the centuries it has been cleared to make way for agriculture and houses and to provide wood. We are very used to being concerned about the disappearance of tropical forest in more recent times without thinking about the destruction wrought in our own country. Even where woods are known to have existed for centuries, they have always been affected by human activity. Great Church Wood is an example. It is known to have existed in 1670 and in recent times was owned by Sir Adrian Boult, the conductor. He sold it to the Forestry Commission, who extracted some mature timber. After a fundraising effort by local people it was bought by the Woodland Trust in 1986 and is a Site of Special Scientific Interest. The fallen timber is a very important part of the habitat, being food for many different invertebrates and fungi. The density of the woods and the confusion of the forest floor makes it obvious why ancient people preferred to travel on the less densely wooded high ground (see Walk 9).

8. Turn left, signed 'South Hawke ¾M', to a fork after 135 yards. Now bear right, this time signed 'South Hawke ½M', and this lovely path leads back to the car park where this walk started.

Walk 20
LINGFIELD

This route is a pleasant, almost level walk exploring the countryside around Lingfield. It uses mainly quiet field paths, not always visible on the ground but easy to follow – if you stick to these directions! Lingfield itself, explored at the start and finish of this walk, has many interesting old buildings. The terrain covered by this route is on Wealden clay, which does not drain freely, as evidenced by the several ponds passed. This means some stretches of path can be muddy after wet weather. The ecology is noticeably different from most of the other walks in this book, which are mainly on the more freely draining chalk and greensand. The vegetation, including nettles, can be lush in summer so shorts are not a good idea.

The biggest challenge on this walk is deciding where to have tea. Bannisters on the A22 near Lingfield, has been a bakery since the 18th century. The ovens, still to be seen, were fed with faggots brought by horse and cart from Dormansland. The firebricks lining the oven heated up and then the ashes were raked out and replaced with dough. Mr and

Mrs Bannister took the bakery over in 1946 and 'Granny Bannie' is still actively involved. The tea rooms opened in 1985 in part of the old bakery and there are also tables outside, some shaded by a pergola. The scones, both sweet and savoury, are outstanding and cream teas include either a cake or cucumber sandwich. There is also an excellent selection of cakes and buns. Possibilities for lunch range from sandwiches to things on toast and full meals. There is a most tempting choice of desserts including brandy bananas served warm with maple syrup and cream. Behind the bakery is a small museum of bakery items. Admission is by token that you buy in the shop. Bannisters is open throughout the year every day except Monday from 9 am, except on Sunday, when they open at 11 am. Last teas are served at 4.30 pm during the week and at 5.30 pm at the weekend. Telephone: 01342 832086.

🍵 Joyce's with Best Wishes on the High Street in Lingfield is your alternative choice for tea. They too offer a very tempting selection of cakes and other teatime goodies with a good choice for lunch too, including excellent omelettes. The sweet menu features delicious meringues served with seasonal fruit or ice cream. The name comes from the fact that they also sell a very wide range of greetings cards and other social stationery with the racks dotted about among the tables – and you might find the hand-made chocolates hard to resist. There is a pleasant garden behind. Joyce's is open every day between 9.15 am and 5.30 pm except Sunday, when it just serves a roast lunch between 12 noon and 2 pm. Telephone: 01342 832428.

DISTANCE: 4½ miles.

MAP: OS Explorer 146 Dorking, Box Hill and Reigate.

STARTING POINT: Gun Pit Road car park, Lingfield (GR 385435).

HOW TO GET THERE: From the B2028 Edenbridge to Crawley road, at the pond in Lingfield take a minor road, Gun Pit Road, to the entrance to the car park on the left.

ALTERNATIVE STARTING POINT: If you wish to visit the teashop at the beginning or end of your walk, start at Bannisters on the A22 about ½ mile south of Blindley Heath, where there is a large car park. You should seek permission before leaving a car for an extended period. You will then start the walk at point 10. As an alternative there is Joyce's with Best Wishes, on the High Street in Lingfield.

THE WALK

1. With your back to the entrance go to the left hand side of the

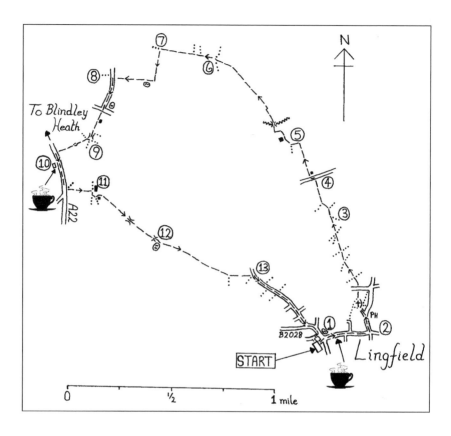

car park and walk through to the main road to emerge at a mini-roundabout. Take the road opposite, signed 'Dormansland Edenbridge'. Walk along the High Street, passing Joyce's with Best Wishes on the right, as far as Church Road on the left.

2. Turn left along Church Road. At the Star bear left past delightful old houses to the church. Take a path to the right of the church round to the rear to find a path down some steps to a road. Cross the road and continue up some steps on the other side to carry on along the path to some wooden gates into a recreation ground. Head straight across the recreation ground to a gap in a hedge then on in the same direction along the right hand side of a field, through another gap and on down to a wooden kissing gate at the bottom left hand corner, giving on to a drive.

3. Turn right along the drive. Follow it round to the right as a track joins from the left to a road.

4. Turn left for 30 yards then right on a hedged path next to Farm Cottage and follow it to a T-junction with a track at a farm.

5. Turn right. Just past the farm bear left on a fenced path round the left hand perimeter of a field to a concrete footbridge. The next part of the route may not be visible on the ground, depending on the time of year, but is waymarked by yellow arrows. Over the bridge, go ahead across a field to a hedge corner then ahead with the hedge on the right to a gap on the right. Go through the gap and turn left to carry on in the same direction, now on the left hand side of a field to a stile. Cross the stile and head across to the far right hand corner of the next field. Now go ahead for about 200 yards to a stile in the hedge on the right giving onto a drive.

6. Turn left for about ¼ mile to a stile on the left into a field. This is unsigned and not obvious.

7. Cross the stile and go ahead across the field to yet another stile, this one beside a gate. Over the stile turn right and walk along the right hand side of a field to a lane.

8. Turn left. At a T-junction take a track directly opposite leading to a house called 'Clacks', where the track ends. Continue ahead on a possibly rather muddy and overgrown path that eventually leads to a concrete bridge.

9. Over the bridge turn right then bear left after 10 yards and press on along a narrow but clear path. Follow the path through a willow hedge onto a track and walk along the track to a main road. Turn left to Bannisters.

Unless the weather has been very dry you will notice how damp it is round here. Blindley Heath Common, owned by the Parish Council, is a Site of Special Scientific Interest as a good example of damp grassland. Until the 18th century it was impossible to get from London to East Grinstead via Blindley Heath in wet weather. Travellers used to wait at Anchor Farm for the ground to dry out and that is the origin of the Blue Anchor Inn in Blindley Heath.

10. Turn right out of the teashop along the road for 200 yards then turn left along the drive to Nestledown Kennels.

11. In front of a large, new house turn right for 25 yards then turn left to pass to the left of an old house, Martyns Platt. Follow the path as it bears round to the right to find a stile next to a field gate. Now walk along the right hand side of a field, across a substantial footbridge and along the left hand side of the next field to yet another stile and a rather broken down (at the time of writing) footbridge over a ditch.

12. A couple of yards on bear right to a pond. Walk along the left hand side of the pond then bear half right across a field to a stile. Now walk along the left hand side of the next field to a stile beside two gates set at 90°. Now head diagonally left across this field and along the left hand side of the next to a road.

13. Turn right and walk into Lingfield. At a mini-roundabout by the Old Cage public house, bear left to the Gun Pond and turn right along Gun Pit Lane back to the start. (Go ahead and left along the High Street if you started at Bannisters.)

Lingfield is a large village of some 7,000 inhabitants best known today for its racecourse. There was a flourishing iron industry here in the 16th century. It went into terminal decline in the 18th century when it supplied guns to France, which was at war with Britain at that time. The Government responded to this lack of patriotism by transferring its contracts to Scotland. The little building next to the pond is the old village cage or lock-up for petty offenders, built in 1773.